The Essentials of
Economic Sustainability

The Essentials of
Economic Sustainability

John Ikerd

Kumarian Press
An Imprint of Stylus Publishing

The Essentials of Economic Sustainability

COPYRIGHT © 2012 by Kumarian Press, an imprint of STYLUS PUBLISHING, LLC.

Published by Stylus Publishing, LLC
22883 Quicksilver Drive
Sterling, Virginia 20166-2102

The text of this book is set in 11/13 Garamond

Editing by Jean B. Bernard
Book design by Nicole Hirschman
Proofread by Kathryn Owens
Index by Robert Swanson

Library of Congress Cataloging-in-Publication Data
Ikerd, John E.
The essentials of economic sustainability / John Ikerd. — 1st ed.
    p.   cm.
    Includes bibliographical references and index.
    ISBN 978-1-56549-515-9 (cloth : alk. paper) — ISBN 978-1-56549-516-6 (pbk. : alk.
    paper) — ISBN 978-1-56549-517-3 (library networkable e-edition) — ISBN
    978-1-56549-518-0 (consumer e-edition)
    1. Sustainable development. 2. Economic development—Environmental aspects. I. Title.
    HC79.E5I4944   2012
    338.9'27—dc23
                                                                            2012000164

13-digit ISBN: 978-1-56549-515-9 (cloth)
13-digit ISBN: 978-1-56549-516-6 (paper)
13-digit ISBN: 978-1-56549-517-3 (library networkable e-edition)
13-digit ISBN: 978-1-56549-518-0 (consumer e-edition)

Printed in the United States of America

All first editions printed on acid-free paper that meets the American National Standards Institute Z39-48 Standard.

Bulk Purchases: Quantity discounts are available for use in workshops and for staff development. Call 1-800-232-0223

First Edition, 2012
10   9   8   7   6   5   4   3   2   1

Contents

Preface

Questions of economic sustainability have received relatively little attention among economists. Most seem to accept the conventional economic assumption that human imagination and creativity are capable of finding a substitute for any resource we humans deplete and finding a solution for any problem we create. All that is needed are the appropriate economic incentives to do so. Even the "ecological economists" seem preoccupied with assigning economic values to the ecological and social consequences of economic decisions. They focus on "internalizing economic externalities." If we "get the prices right," the markets will ensure sustainability. Few economists seem willing to face the reality that all economic value is ultimately derived from nature and society, both of which are inevitably degraded and depleted by economic activity. Economic incentives, by their very nature, are inherently inadequate to ensure the continual investments in resource renewal and regeneration that are necessary to economic sustainability. Assigning market values to the economic contributions of nature and society fails to address the innate inability of markets to ensure economic sustainability.

Investments based on *noneconomic* social and ethical values are absolutely essential to ensure economic sustainability. To meet the needs of the present without diminishing opportunities for the future, people must act, both individually and collectively, to protect and promote the greater common good of society and humanity. No single book is likely to change the minds of many economists regarding authentic sustainability. Thus, this book was written primarily for the benefit of noneconomists. Nothing in this book is in conflict with fundamental economic theory; it just doesn't conform to current economic dogma. It addresses the ecological, social, and economic essentials of economic sustainability from ethical, societal, and individual perspectives. It does not rely on the decrees of renowned economists of liberal or conservative inclinations but instead on logic and reason to reveal ecological, social, and economic reality. It addresses essential economic principles without resorting to economic jargon. Formal course work in economics may be either an asset or an obstacle, depending on the willingness of readers to think for themselves.

This is a very short book covering a very broad topic. Economic sustainability is a holistic concept. It cannot be understood in parts but, instead, must be understood as a whole. The book is long enough to address all of the essentials of economic sustainability without being so long as to discourage even the casual reader with an interest in the economic dimension of sustainability. Although the book is short, it is highly flexible and almost infinitely expandable. It can be a weekend read for an individual or can be expanded into a series of group discussions spread over a period of several weeks. It can fit nicely into a three-day workshop or be expanded into a full course for academic credit. It can serve as either a supplementary or primary text for a course in economic sustainability at the advanced high school, undergraduate, or graduate levels.

The flexibility and expandability of the book arises from its reliance on a collaborative or co-learning approach to education. The reader must accept major responsibility for whatever learning or knowledge he or she gains from this book. No references are provided to support specific conclusions. Readers, group leaders, or instructors must seek out relevant references to support or refute conclusions they feel require additional verification or that seem subject to refutation. No specific current examples are provided to show specific applications of general principles or concepts. The reader, group leader, or instructor must come up with appropriate examples to illustrate applications of concept and principles whenever there may be a need for amplification. Suggestions regarding references and examples are at the end of each chapter. An annotated bibliography also provides additional readings relevant to the subjects covered in each chapter.

There is also a series of questions at the end of each chapter that addresses some of the key issues covered in that chapter. These questions are meant to encourage readers to integrate the essential principles and concepts of economic sustainability into their own systems of thinking. A person may be able to quote extensively from what others have written or said, but people have not truly learned anything until they claim it as their own. Readers may well find things in the book they do not and cannot believe and thus choose not to integrate into their own thinking. However, they can never be confident in their own truth unless they are willing to challenge it with the truth of others. True learning is a collaborative process between writer and reader, between teacher and student. This book asks the reader to do his or her part in this process. For some readers, this short book might well represent the beginning of a lifelong process of co-learning.

This book is intentionally limited in scope to the basic principles and concepts of economic sustainability, without regard to the political or economic philosophies of the people of nations that might choose to apply them. Some of these concepts are capitalist, some are socialistic, and others are general principles validated by philosophy or common sense. All current economies are mixed economies; they have aspects of both market and planned economies. Thus the essential characteristics of markets and essential roles of governments are addressed. This new synthesis of principles and concepts results in an economic system that is neither capitalist nor socialist but something fundamentally different; it is sustainable.

This book is written in the most basic, concise, straightforward English possible to facilitate its translation into other languages. Its lack of specific references to any other works, economic or otherwise, is also an attempt to minimize any political or cultural bias. The objective is to maximize the book's acceptance in all countries and cultures of the world. It is an attempt to synthesize a set of core ecological, social, economic, and philosophical principles into a comprehensive and coherent economic paradigm that can guide the quest for economic sustainability by individuals, organizations, and governments in any part of the world at any level or stage of economic development.

Acknowledgments

I will not attempt to name all of the people who have contributed directly to the thinking reflected in this book. A few of the many authors from whom I have learned are mentioned in the annotated bibliography. I have learned from countless other thoughtful individuals by various means on numerous occasions at a wide variety of different venues over the years. They have been far too many to recount here, and most probably don't realize they have contributed to my understanding. This book is just the most recent publication reflecting a lifetime of learning influenced by virtually everyone I have ever known and everything I have ever read or experienced.

That being said, I do want to thank Lonnie Gamble for helping me to clarify some of the basic concepts in this book, including the collaborative approach to learning, while we were co-teaching a course in economic sustainability at Maharishi University of Management. I also want to express my appreciation to those who have provided opportunities for me to share the ideas in this book with students, academics, and professionals in several different countries. Finally, I want to thank my wife, Ellen, who has read virtually every word I have written for the past dozen-plus years, and has read, reviewed, and proofed this particular manuscript several times. Without her support and encouragement, this book would not have been possible. Together, I hope we may have made a contribution to a clearer understanding of the essentials of economic sustainability.

The Essential Questions of Economic Sustainability

The Great Transformation

The world is continually changing. In fact, change is said to be "the only constant in life." Thus, change is a normal and usual aspect of life. However, some changes are not normal or usual. Some are truly revolutionary. In fact, every few hundred years throughout human history, societies have gone through great transformations, and there are growing indications that humanity is currently undergoing another such revolutionary change. The transformation taking place today may be at least as important as the Industrial Revolution of the late 1700s and perhaps as important as the beginning of interest in science in the early 1600s. Such changes come about when people are forced to rethink their ideas about how the world works and how we humans fit within it. Such revolutions in thinking eventually change virtually every aspect of human life. The current transformation is being driven by questions of sustainability: How can we meet the needs of the present without diminishing opportunities for the future?

This is also the essential question of economic sustainability: How can we meet the *economic* needs of the present without diminishing *economic* opportunities for the future? An economy that fails to meet the basic economic needs of its people is inherently unstable and potentially volatile, politically and economically. Such an economy is not sustainable. Sustainability does not require everyone to have everything he or she wants. It does require everyone to have adequate food, shelter, clothing, and the other essentials to meet his or her basic needs for physical and mental development and well-being. Furthermore, in meeting the basic economic needs of all in the present, a sustainable economy must not deprive future generations of opportunities to meet their basic economic needs as well. A sustainable economy must be able to maintain its productivity and value to society indefinitely, essentially forever.

Energy: The Ultimate Source of All Economic Value

Things have economic value only if they are functional or useful to people. All things that are useful to people are derived ultimately from nature and society. Economies are not capable of *creating* anything of value; they simply facilitate the process of extracting things of value from natural and human resources. Furthermore, all physical things of use to people—food, lodging, clothing, transportation—require energy to make and energy to use. In fact, all material things are simply concentrated forms of energy. In addition, all useful human activities—working, managing, thinking, creating—also require energy, specifically biological energy. About one-fifth of the total energy the human body uses is required just to fuel the brain. Economic sustainability ultimately depends on the sustainable use of energy.

According to the first law of thermodynamics, energy can neither be created nor destroyed. Thus, sustainability might seem inevitable. However, each time energy is used to do anything useful, some portion of its usefulness is lost. This is the second law of thermodynamics—the law of entropy. The loss of usefulness to entropy is inevitable and unavoidable. Whenever energy is used to do something useful, what physicists call *work,* its form invariably changes. Specifically, it changes from more-concentrated, more-organized forms to less-concentrated, less-organized forms, as when gasoline is ignited in the engine of an automobile. When the gasoline explodes, energy is simply expressing its natural tendency to dissipate and disorganize whenever it is disturbed. This natural tendency to change from concentrated, organized forms to dispersed, disorganized forms gives energy its ability to perform work—to be useful to people.

Energy isn't destroyed by use, as is stated in the first law of thermodynamics. However, each time energy is used and reused it becomes less concentrated, less organized, and thus less useful than before. Eventually all energy becomes useless; it loses its potential to do anything useful, and thus to produce anything of economic value. This is an inevitable and undeniable result of the physical law of entropy. An economy that depends on *nonrenewable* sources of energy, most notably fossil energy, is not sustainable. Beyond some point, its ability to produce things of economic value will diminish and eventually will be lost. Even as such an economy continues to grow, the energy needed to meet the needs of future generations is unavoidably diminishing and will be depleted eventually.

The only source of energy available to offset the unavoidable loss of useful energy is solar energy, the daily inflow of energy from the sun. Thus, a sustainable economy must capture and store sufficient quantities of solar energy to offset the loss of useful energy, including the unavoidable loss of usefulness due to entropy. Currently available forms of solar energy include heat captured by various types of passive solar collectors as well as electricity generated by photovoltaic cells. Generation of electricity by wind and water is also sustained by solar heating of the earth's atmosphere. The solar energy captured and stored by photosynthetic processes of green plants and other living organisms is of specific concern for sustainability, as it is essential for life. Life on Earth, including human life, cannot be sustained without adequate energy from biological sources in addition to other forms of solar energy.

The Economic Productivity of Society

Economic productivity depends on the capacity of people to transform the physical energy available from nature into forms that are functional and useful to humans. The amount of economic value a society is able to extract from a given amount of physical energy ultimately depends on the capabilities of its people—its human resources. However, no amount of human imagination, creativity, or innovation can eliminate the ultimate reliance of economic value on physical energy. People cannot create energy; they can only make whatever energy is available, including solar energy, more useful to humans. The economy is simply a means of facilitating this process. In addition, people are not economically useful when they are born; they are helpless infants. They must be nurtured, educated, socialized, and civilized for many years before they reach their full capacity as economically productive individuals. Many of these capacity-building functions are beyond individual capabilities. They must be performed by families, communities, and societies. It takes energy to produce productive people, including societal or social energy.

Social energy may be defined as the energy expended in maintaining positive, productive, human relationships. Positive relationships require physical and mental energy. Humans, as fallible beings, invariably degrade and deplete the quality of their social relationships through unavoidable mistakes, unintentional neglect, and avoidable abuse—a kind of "social entropy." Thus, social energy is inevitably depleted through use. Relationships within families, communities, and societies require energy to maintain, energy to restore, and energy to replace. An economy that fails to invest sufficient energy in renewing and regenerating society is not sustainable, no matter how much physical energy it may conserve, renew, or regenerate.

Differences Between Economic and Social Values

Economies are not absolutely necessary. However, the only alternative to an economy is self-sufficiency. Once individuals decide to barter with someone else to get something they otherwise would have had to obtain from nature themselves, they have formed an economic relationship and created a microcosm of an economy. Families, communities, and societies are not absolutely necessary. However, the only alternative to such social relationships is individual isolation. Once an individual decides to relate to another person for purposes other than getting something from nature, that individual has formed a social relationship and created a microcosm of a society. Economic and social relationships are both essential for economic sustainability.

Economic relationships are individual, instrumental, and impersonal. Economic value is *individual* in that it accrues to individuals and not to families, communities, or societies as wholes. An economy is nothing more or less than a collection of individual economic enterprises and organizations. Economic relationships are *instrumental* because they are an instrument or means for achieving some further end, specifically, a means of acquiring something of economic value in return. As a result, the value of an economic relationship is always deferred until something of economic value is received in return. Sometimes the expected economic value is realized almost instantly, and sometimes it is deferred for months or years. Finally, economic relationships are *impersonal* because something of economic value acquired from one person is no different from something of equal economic value acquired from another person. Consequently, anything of economic value received from one person can always be exchanged with or traded to someone else.

Social value is also individual and instrumental but is not impersonal. Social relationships are instrumental in that social value depends on reciprocity or the expectation of something in return. The reciprocal expectation may not be specific with respect to what or when something might be expected. For example, those who expect to have a friend must also be a friend, although what is expected from a friendship may be difficult to define. Even though instrumental, the value of social relationships is not economic because social relationships are clearly personal in nature. A social relationship with one person is fundamentally different from a social relationship with another person, even if both are friends, family members, or neighbors. Relationships that are purely social are personally unique or person-specific and thus cannot be exchanged or traded to another person.

Unlike economic relationships, social relationships produce no "marketable" goods or services. Thus, the value of purely social relationships cannot be "internalized" or transformed into marketable products. The value of personal relationships is experienced only as long as individuals remain personally connected or in the relationship. Once a purely personal relationship ends, its value disappears; there is no product left that can be traded, rented, or sold to anyone else. Social values are clearly different from economic values.

Uniqueness of Ethical Value

Ethical relationships differ from both economic and social relationships in that ethical relationships are noninstrumental and impersonal. Actions that are purely ethical in nature are not an instrument or means of acquiring some further ends. Consequently, the benefits of ethical behavior are immediate, rather than deferred. Even those who expect to be rewarded for their ethical deeds in some afterlife do not expect to receive anything of economic or social value. Religions that promise personal wealth or social success as a consequence of righteous living are in the business of economics or politics rather than morality or ethics. Purely ethical relationships produce nothing of economic value that can be exchanged with or traded to anyone else. Ethical relationships are clearly noneconomic. Unlike social relationships, purely ethical relationships show no preference for specific individuals or persons—they are not personally discriminatory. What is ethically right or wrong in a relationship with one person is right or wrong in relationships with any other person, in both the present and the future.

Ethical values are a particular culture's interpretation of morality. Morality is an abstract universal code of conduct, once commonly referred to as "natural law," that applies to all people of all times. The ethical values of a particular culture may or may not actually be moral because the laws of human nature are not perfectly knowable. A cultural ethic reflects a particular culture's imperfect knowledge of nature's laws.

Ethical values naturally evolve from social values. Cultural knowledge or wisdom evolves over time from a society's collective experience of personal social relationships. Principles that previous experience has shown to be essential to personal relationships in friendships and within families are extended to less personal relationships among neighbors within communities. As social relationships become less personal, people begin to understand that the social values they experience as individuals are relevant not just to their personal connections but to all personal interconnectedness within families, communities, and societies as wholes. Values they discover to be right and good in their personal relationships are deemed to be right and good in all human relationships. This is the process by which personal social values evolve to impersonal ethical values.

Differences Among Types of Value Matter

At first thought, this distinction among economic, social, and ethical relationships and values may seem academic or trivial, but it is not. All claims that market economies serve the collective economic interest of society are based on the assumption that people attempt to maximize their individual, impersonal, instrumental economic self-interests. In cases where this assertion is not true, economists have no rational or logical means of deriving conclusions regarding the performance of market economies. To the extent that a relationship is purely personal, it is not economic and thus not subject to economic interpretations. Certainly, some social and ethical relationships also have economic value, but some values are purely social and ethical. Social relationships can create economic value by facilitating economic relationships—which economists refer to as "reducing transactions costs." Ethical relationships also can create economic value, in that many people prefer to do business with individuals and organizations whose ethical values they share. However, to the extent that relationships are purely personal, they are social rather than economic or ethical. To the extent that relationships are noninstrumental and impersonal, they are ethical rather than social or economic. To the extent that value is created by relationships that are personal and noninstrumental, it is not economic value.

Economists freely admit that people do things for social and ethical reasons and accept the logic of doing so. They rationalize that all such actions in fact are economic because they somehow benefit the individual in some instrumental and impersonal way. Market economists also admit that some economic costs and benefits are not reflected in market prices. They label such values as "external" and suggest various means of "internalizing externalities" so markets will reflect all relevant social and ecological values. They fail to recognize that purely social or ethical values simply cannot be exchanged or transferred from one person to another; they have no *economic* value to internalize. Economics as an academic discipline steadfastly refuses to recognize the existence of any uniquely social or ethical values that cannot be converted into economic value or at least measured in economic terms.

Emergent Properties of Societies and Economies

Social benefits obviously accrue to individuals. However, friendships, families, communities, and societies have emergent properties that make them something more than simply collections of individuals—relationships matter. Furthermore, as social consciousness evolves, people tend to become more cooperative as they come to appreciate their interdependence with the larger whole or the common good. They begin to understand and act upon their inherent sense of interconnectedness with society and humanity as a whole. The emergent properties of social relationships evolve into an ethical commitment to protect, preserve, and promote the common good and the good of the commons, a commitment that is essential for economic sustainability.

Social values, such as honesty, fairness, responsibility, respect, and compassion among friends and neighbors, evolve into ethical commitments to social equity and justice "for all people." The ethical values needed to sustain positive personal relationships among current generations evolve into commitments to equity and justice for future generations as well. Since ethical values are impersonal, they can be extended as well to relationships with nonpersons—to earth, air, water, forests, lakes, streams, rocks, or other species. Thus, ethical commitments to stewardship of nature evolve from relationships with nature as well as relationships among humans. Economic sustainability is an emergent property of trusting, caring relationships.

Economies also have emergent properties. However, the aggregate value of an economy is simply the sum of economic worth of the individual enterprises that make up the economy. Emergent properties have economic value only to the extent that market values of the individual economic enterprises reflect the economic integrity of an overall economy. For example, the value of corporate stocks may be affected by the overall strength of the economy. However, individual enterprises have little economic incentive to invest in protecting, preserving, or promoting the integrity of overall economies. This is the classic example of a "tragedy of the commons." Individuals and entities motivated solely by economic self-interest have no incentive to protect the productivity of the commons, in this case the economy, from which they derive their economic well-being. The global economic crisis of 2008 was a classic example of financial firms having no individual incentive to protect the overall integrity of the economy from which they derived their economic returns.

Furthermore, as economic consciousness evolves, individuals tend to become more competitive and focus more narrowly on their individual economic self-interests. At some point, a growing preoccupation with economic relationships actually may begin to degrade and destroy social and ethical relationships necessary for economic sustainability.

Rational and Irrational Economic Decisions

It seems obvious to most noneconomists that rational people routinely make decisions based on considerations that are not solely economic in nature. They do things for family members, friends, neighbors, and society with no expectation of receiving anything of economic value in return. Human beings are social beings. People need personal relationships with other people and need to feel a sense of connectedness to human communities, for reasons distinct and apart from any economic value they might receive in return. Humans also are ethical beings. People need an ethical sense of rightness and goodness in their relationships with nature and with other people, for reasons that are completely separate from purely economic or social interests. Individuals vary widely in their willingness to allow social and ethical values to affect their decisions, but rational people make logical decisions that are not economic in nature.

Unlike people, organizations dedicated to purely economic purposes have no capacity to form or express purely social or ethical values. They make rational economic decisions. Most important, the corporations that dominate today's global economy epitomize this type of organization. Most of these organizations are large, multinational, for-profit, publicly traded corporations. They are legally obligated to serve the common interests of their stockholders. The stockholders of many such corporations are scattered around the world, representing a wide variety of nationalities, cultures, religions, and philosophies. As a result, the thousands or millions of owners of such corporations have no *common* social or ethical values. Their only commonly held value is their desire to enhance the economic value of their individual investments, either through corporate dividends or appreciation in market value of corporate stocks.

The managers of such corporations are obligated by law to serve the common interest of their companies' shareholders. They are obligated to make purely economic decisions. They have neither the capacity nor the legal responsibility to make purely social or ethical decisions for the benefit of society or humanity. Such corporations obviously make investments and decisions that result in economic benefits for individual members of society and humanity. However, any contributions they make to the well-being of families, communities, societies, or humanity are preconditioned on the expectation of realizing something of greater economic value in return. Such corporations are the epitome of the rational "economic individual" of economic theory.

Economic Priority of the Present

The individual, instrumental, and impersonal nature of economic value is of particular relevance to questions of economic sustainability. It makes no economic sense to invest in anything for the sole benefit of anyone else or solely for the benefit of a society or humanity. Thus, a market economy provides no incentives to meet the basic economic needs of *all* people within a society. An economy will respond only to the needs of those who can offer something of greater economic value in return. In addition, it makes no economic sense to invest in anything for the sole benefit of some future generation. It is economically irrational to make an investment if the expected return is deferred until after the investor's death. Since life is inherently uncertain, economic value places a premium on the present over the future. The needs of future generations are given little, if any, economic consideration.

Economic value always discounts future values relative to present values. The promise of receiving a smaller economic return next week or next month may be far more valuable than the promise of receiving a larger return deferred until the next year or next decade. For these reasons many consumers willingly pay interest when they borrow money; it's worth more economically to spend the money sooner rather than wait until later. This is also the reason people expect interest when they lend money; they expect to be compensated for deferring the use of money they could have used sooner and now wait until sometime later. People will save and invest money, rather than spend it, only if they believe the value of their investment will increase by enough over time to more than offset the declining economic value of each dollar or unit of money invested. They will naturally give priority to investments that promise quicker returns over those for which returns are deferred further into the future. Investments expected to yield more products more quickly represent greater value to potential buyers.

For example, at an interest rate of 7 percent, a given amount of money ten years in the future is worth only half as much as the same amount of money today . . . because money invested at a compounded interest rate of 7 percent will double in value in ten years. A given monetary payoff expected to accrue one hundred years in the future has less than 1/1000th of the economic value of the same amount of money received today. If a return on an investment is not expected to accrue until some future generation, the economic value of even a very large payoff or return may be insignificantly small. Obviously, such investments cannot compete successfully with investments promising positive returns next week, next year, or even next decade. At a corporate rate of return of 15 percent, values of investments double every five years, which discounts expected future returns even more. This is why many corporate planning horizons extend only five to seven years into the future.

Well-meaning economists perpetuate the myth that all that is needed to address the issue of sustainability is to do things that make good "long-run economic sense." The problem is that economies invariably place a priority on the present over the future. What is good for the economic organizations over the long run is fundamentally different from what makes economic sense to the people who are managing economic organizations today. Economic decisions are always based on "present values," not "future values." Costs and returns expected in the future are always "discounted" to derive "net present values." This gives decision makers equivalent values by which to compare the expected income streams between investments with shorter- and longer-term payoff periods. So the needs of future generations are never given anything approaching equal consideration when decisions are based on economic value.

Economic Incentives for Sustainability

The people who manage large corporate economic organizations may be socially and ethically responsible people. In many cases they may be able to make economic decisions that benefit society and nature and may gladly choose to do so whenever possible. However, there is an inherent conflict between economic profit or growth and economic sustainability. This conflict becomes apparent once the opportunities to do things that have economic value as well as social and ethical values have been exploited. In such cases, which are most common in today's global economy, the corporate manager's responsibility is to choose profits and growth over economic sustainability.

People can make noneconomic decisions that reflect their social and ethical commitments to sustainability. Such decisions make it possible for economic organizations to gain economic value by responding to such noneconomic decisions of their customers. For example, consumers who are willing to pay premium prices for products that are produced by sustainable means provide economic incentives for sustainable production. While this moves a society closer to sustainability, economic organizations still have economic incentives to exploit the noneconomic vulnerabilities of their customers. For example, they may be able to charge higher prices for so-called "sustainable products" that are produced by unsustainable means. Even if such exploitation eventually discredits the organization and causes it to fail economically, the discounted net present value of its long-run economic demise might not be as great as the value of the exploitative short-run profits. Exploitation of misinformed borrowers was a rational economic contributor to the collapse of large financial institutions and the global financial crisis of 2008. To ensure economic sustainability, society must impose constraints on economic exploitation.

Economies that respond solely to market incentives will not meet the needs of all in the present, nor will they ensure equal opportunities for future generations. Economies guided solely by economic incentives are not resilient, regenerative, or self-sustaining, regardless of market economists' claims to the contrary. Economic incentives alone are inherently inadequate to ensure the long-term investments in nature and society that are absolutely necessary for economic sustainability. Economic trends of the past several decades have validated this proposition. As economies have become increasingly dominated by large, multinational corporations, the negative environmental, social, and economic consequences have become more readily apparent. The "speculative bubbles" in global stock markets in the 1990s and in financial markets in the 2000s were attempts to create economic illusions to mask the reality of declining real economic productivity due to depletion and degradation of natural and human resources. Economies guided solely by economic values are inherently extractive and exploitative; such economies are not sustainable.

Social and Ethical Incentives for Sustainability

All economic value must be derived from nature and society. Thus, the question of economic sustainability is inseparable from questions of ecological and social sustainability. If nature and society are not sustainable, neither is the economy. The economy is but a means by which people meet their individual, instrumental, impersonal needs. Meeting the economic needs of individuals is undeniably important and essential to economic sustainability. However, economic value is of no more importance than are social and ethical values in ensuring economic sustainability.

Sustainable economies must make the economic investments necessary to meet the needs of both current and future generations. Furthermore, they must generate an economic surplus to support the noneconomic investments necessary for economic sustainability. Individuals must be able to do more than meet their individual needs to contribute socially or ethically to their communities and humanity. Economies likewise must do more than simply meet the needs of individuals to contribute to the social and ethical well-being of society. An economy that cannot sustain itself clearly cannot contribute to the greater good of society and humanity.

However, an economy cannot sustain itself in the absence of essential noneconomic investments. Decisions and actions based solely on social and ethical values are absolutely necessary to ensure the long-term economic investments in society and nature that are essential for ecological, social, and economic sustainability. Unlike economic values, social values create a sense of connectedness or commonality and evolve into the ethical values necessary for sustainability. Unlike economic values, the value of ethical decisions is immediate, not deferred. It makes ethical sense to do things solely for the benefit of other people, including those of both current and future generations. People need not be bribed with economic incentives to do the things necessary to ensure economic sustainability. Potential social and ethical values are adequate to justify sustainable public choices and individual lifestyles. People only lack the awareness and the willingness to challenge the dogma of economic self-interests. They simply need to learn to balance the basic economic, social, and ethical dimensions of human well-being in choosing a sustainable way of life. This is the challenge of economic sustainability.

This is a time of fundamental change. People all around the world are asking: How can we meet the economic needs of the present without compromising economic opportunities for the future? People increasingly are questioning the blind faith of market economists that competitive markets will somehow transform individual self-interests into the common interests of society and humanity. Increasingly, people are coming to the logical and rational conclusion that economies dominated by economic self-interests are not sustainable.

A sustainable economy must provide permanent sustenance for the individual, social, and ethical well-being of all, including those in the future. It must enhance the physical and mental health of individuals. It must promote the economic and social health of families, communities, and societies. It must sustain the productivity and ecological health of nature. And it must provide each generation with the means of fulfilling its ethical responsibilities for the future of humanity. Questions of how to balance the economic, social, and ethical incentives needed to create such economies are the essential questions of economic sustainability.

Study and Discussion Guide for Individual Readers and Group Leaders or Instructors

- Search the Internet or a library for at least two timely and culturally appropriate references for economic sustainability. Each reference should include at least one supporting corporate responsibility as a means of ensuring economic sustainability and at least one supporting government regulations as being necessary for sustainability.
- Identify at least two current examples of public issues or controversies that relate to questions of economic sustainability. The examples should include one local or national issue and one global issue.
- Trace the economic values of a specific physical item and a specific personal service back to their original sources in nature, society, and, ultimately, to energy.

Questions for Individual Reflection or Group Discussion

- What is your definition of *economic sustainability*?
- Do you believe sustainable use of energy is essential to economic sustainability? Why or why not?
- Do you believe economic value is fundamentally different from social and ethical value? Why or why not?
- Do you believe the decisions of large, publicly traded corporate organizations are different from the decisions of real people? Why or why not?
- Do you believe government regulations are essential for economic sustainability? Why or why not?
- Why are your answers to these questions important to the people of your nation and your community and to you personally?
- After thinking about these questions, what might you do differently to make life better, for others and for yourself?

2

The Essential Hierarchies
of Economic Sustainability

A Question of Worldviews

Most economists limit their concerns about sustainability to the intersection of or overlap among the conceptual spheres of nature, society, and economy. The implicit assumption is that whatever else happens within society or nature is of no economic value and thus is of no relevance to economic sustainability. Only those economic decisions and actions that affect the capacity of nature and society to produce things of economic value are considered relevant to economic sustainability. This economic worldview leaves major portions of the economy, society, and nature outside the area or intersection of common concern, so they are of no relevance to questions of economic sustainability.

The essential questions of sustainability arise from a clearly different worldview. From the worldview of authentic sustainability, the whole of human society is contained within the realm of nature and the whole of the economy exists within the realm of society and thus the economy is also within the realm of nature. All parts of human society are also parts of nature. All aspects of the economy are also aspects of human society. Thus, the whole of the economy intersects and overlaps with both society and nature. Every economic action affects both society and nature. Every economic decision has social and ecological "externalities," not just some small subset of economic decisions. Every social decision likewise affects nature, because humans are a part of nature. This worldview is fundamentally different from the contemporary economic worldview; it is, however, the worldview essential to economic sustainability.

Hierarchy of Sustainability: Nature, Society, and Economy

The relationships among nature, society, and the economy are hierarchal. Nature represents a higher organizational level or plane than society and society represents a higher level of organization than the economy. This ordinal ranking or hierarchy is derived from a distinction between purpose and possibilities. The purposes of lower levels of organization are always derived from higher levels of organization and the possibilities of higher levels are always dependent on lower levels of organization. Purpose is essential to give meaning to possibilities.

The organizational structure of the human body can be thought of as complex systems of nested hierarchies. The whole of the body is analogous to nature, the blood circulation system is analogous to society, and the heart is analogous to the economy. The purpose of the heart is to pump blood through the circulatory system, which in turn provides oxygen and nutrients to the rest of the body. The heart has a distinct function but it has no purpose apart from the circulatory system, its next higher level of organization. The circulatory system likewise has a distinct function, but its purpose is derived from the body as a whole, its next higher level of organization. Thus, the ultimate purpose of the heart is to help the circulatory system keep the whole body alive and healthy. Apart from sustaining the life of the body, the heart and circulatory system have no purpose.

Possibilities of the higher levels of organization depend on the lower levels of organization. If the heart fails to perform its function, the circulatory system will be unable to keep the body alive. If the heart muscle grows weak with age, the health of the whole body is affected; its possibilities are diminished. Even if only a few arteries in the circulatory system become partially blocked, the health of the body is affected; its possibilities are diminished. The possibilities of the body depend on the functioning of all the lower levels in the body's organizational hierarchy. However, these possibilities have no relevance, significance, or meaning apart from their purpose. The possibilities of the heart don't matter if the body is dying because of the failure of some other essential function.

Higher Levels Define Purpose, Lower Levels Affect Possibilities

Returning to the hierarchy of nature, society, and economy, the purpose of the economy must be derived from society, and the purpose of society must be derived from nature. This raises the question of whether the earth, societies, or individuals actually have purposes. Modern science considers all living and nonliving things to be merely consequences of meaningless chemical, electrical, and biological processes occurring within a pointlessly expanding universe. Regardless, most people behave or act as if their lives have purpose. If life had no purpose, there would be no reason to do or not to do anything. There would be no means to defining good or bad and right or wrong. There would be no reason to be concerned about the well-being of others or the future of humanity. Without purpose, life simply makes no sense. Regardless, if human society has purpose, it must be derived from nature, and if an economy has purpose, it must be derived from society, which means the purpose of the economy also is derived from nature.

The possibilities of societies are clearly affected by economies, and the possibilities of nature are clearly affected by human societies. Growing evidence of natural resource depletion and environmental degradation are clear signs that economies and societies affect the possibilities of nature, even if only negatively. Admittedly, some legitimate questions arise regarding the ability of economies and human societies to enhance or expand the possibilities of nature. At the very least, since they are parts of nature, the health and vitality of economies and societies quite logically are aspects of the health and vitality of nature. At some point, all analogies fail. Whereas the human body cannot survive without a heart or circulatory system, nature quite likely could survive without humans or their economies. The quest for economic sustainability is an attempt to avoid testing the truth of this proposition.

Higher Levels Change More Slowly

Higher organizational levels act more slowly and thus change more slowly than do the lower levels within nested hierarchies. Significant changes in nature evolve over eras or eons, whereas human society can make measurable progress or regress within centuries. Economies may fluctuate dramatically decade-to-decade or even year-to-year. As explained in chapter 1, economic incentives are essentially limited to a single life span and diminish dramatically even within a single decade. The negative impacts of the economy on society may not become readily apparent until decades and perhaps even centuries of economic exploitation have occurred. The full negative impacts of an economically exploitative society may not become readily apparent in nature for centuries or even millennia. Even after the degradation becomes clear, a society may require decades even to begin to change, and then centuries before societal changes begin to reverse the degradation of nature. Both society and nature are living systems. At some point, damage to living system becomes irreversible—sustainability is then no longer possible. Societies clearly cannot wait for economic incentives to motivate the changes needed to ensure economic sustainability.

Higher Levels Are Stronger

Fortunately, higher levels in nested hierarchies have greater integrity and strength than do lower levels. Societies clearly can be damaged and even destroyed by continued economic exploitation. However, societies can endure significant economic abuse without losing their ability to regain control and restore integrity to their economies. Human societies also are capable of doing significant damage to nature, even if they cannot destroy it. However, nature has far greater strength and integrity than does humanity. Even if societies were to allow economic exploitation to make the earth uninhabitable by humans, nature would likely endure the loss and eventually restore its ecological integrity. This proposition has not yet been tested, for which we are thankful. Despite obvious signs of ecological and societal degradation, there is still hope for restoring the integrity of nature and society and creating a sustainable economy; nature is strong and resilient.

Higher Levels Set Limits

Higher levels in the organizational hierarchy define limits or constraints within which lower-level organizations must function. As is now obvious, the resources of nature upon which human societies ultimately depend are both finite in quantity and limited in flow or availability. The ultimate ability of nature to support human societies and human life in general is finite and absolute, even if it is still unknown. More efficient technologies and methodologies may expand the usefulness of limited natural resources, but the capacity of human societies to produce things of economic value from nature is nonetheless finite and absolute. The precise limits of sustainable economic development are unknown, but we do know them to be finite or limited.

Market economists implicitly deny the existence of finite limits to economic growth. Human needs and wants are considered to be insatiable and humans are assumed to have an infinite capacity to create things of economic value. Human creativity and innovation are considered to be capable of solving any social or ecological problem created by economic exploitation. Human initiative and entrepreneurship are assumed capable of finding a substitute for any resource depleted by economic extraction. Economists routinely deny or ignore the finite limits nature places on society. However, denial and ignorance do not create economic reality. The economy is contained wholly and completely within the bounds of society and nature. The economy has no other sources of energy to create anything of economic value. Nature and society represent finite sources of energy, which are subject to the law of entropy.

Higher Levels Define Principles

Perhaps most important, higher levels within nested hierarchies define the principles or laws by which all lower levels function. Nature, being the highest level, defines the principles by which both societies and economies function. For example, the law of gravity obviously is relevant to both societies and economics. As with other laws of nature, we can ignore or deny gravity, but we cannot avoid its consequences. The living systems of nature, including societies and economies, also function according to basic principles of natural ecosystems, such as holism, diversity, and interdependence. Perhaps less obvious are the natural principles of human relationships, which include trust, kindness, and courage. The most basic principles of economics are the natural principles of individual human behavior, including scarcity, efficiency, and sovereignty.

The essential ecological, social, and economic principles of sustainability are discussed in detail in chapters 3, 4, and 5. Since economies are created by societies, economies may be required to function according to additional values defined by the societies that create them. These additional social values may be evaluated periodically, renegotiated, and redefined. The principles of nature, however, are unchanging. The principles by which nature functions are not arbitrary or negotiable. Principles, or natural laws, are not created by humans; humans only discover them. They may be ignored or denied, but the laws of nature ultimately will prevail in all societies and economies.

Since all aspects of nature, society, and the economy are ultimately interconnected, as is discussed in depth in chapter 3, principles that tend to be associated specifically with nature, society, or economics are relevant also to all aspects of all levels within the hierarchy of sustainability. Principles typically associated with economics also are relevant to relationships within society and with nature; principles typically associated with social relationships also are relevant to economic and ecological relationships; and principles typically associated with natural ecosystems are relevant also to societies and economies. The basic laws of nature are relevant to everything everywhere.

The Uniqueness of Human Intentionality

Among the living elements of nature, humans are of unique importance, at least to the sustainability of humanity. Humans have the capacity for thoughtful, purposeful, intentional decisions and actions. They have the ability to temper or restrain their innate, instinctive, animalistic urges for self-gratification, survival, and reproduction. Some other species also have social tendencies that restrain or condition their individual self-interest. However, only humans are capable of deliberate acts motivated solely by interest other than social or self-interests. They have the capacity to make purely ethical or moral decisions. Humans also have the mental capacity to anticipate the consequences of actions they have never observed or experienced. Many species are capable of learning but only through experience or parental guidance. No other species is capable of developing abstract models of the potential consequences of novel events that have never occurred anywhere at any time in the past. No other species is capable of anticipating the ultimate demise of its own species, if it continues to pursue a specific course of action.

Other species occasionally find themselves in positions of dominance in their natural environment. Their natural tendency is to continue reproducing and expanding their populations until they deplete the resources needed for their survival—until their populations collapse. Alternatively, overcrowding may result in diseases or physical conflicts that reduce their populations back to preexpansion levels, or even to the level of extinction. The human species now finds itself in a position of dominance over the entire global ecosystem. Some people argue that humans are no different fundamentally from any other animal. If these skeptics are correct, there is no hope for economic sustainability. If humans lack the capacity to anticipate the consequences of their actions or the ability to restrain their animalistic urges, their species will suffer the same fate as other species in similar positions. Persistent resource extraction and societal exploitation will lead to a collapse in human population and perhaps to extinction of the human species. Alternatively, overcrowding may lead to resource wars and disease epidemics that reduce global population to some preexpansion level. Even if humanity survives, its primitive societies and economies of the future will bear little resemblance to those of today.

A precondition for economic sustainability is the uniquely human capacities for self-determination and intentionality. Societies can choose either to respect or disrespect the laws of nature, including human nature, in their pursuit of individual economic self-interests. People can choose to pursue only their narrow individual economic self-interests or can consider the broader interests of society and of humanity in their decisions and actions. Humans are capable of tempering and moderating their undeniably animalistic nature. Individuals can restrain their consumption and limit their reproduction, not only for their own benefit but also for the greater good of their society and of humanity. They can choose to meet their own needs in ways that do not diminish opportunities for others in their societies or for those of future generations. The challenges of economic sustainability can be met, but only through the intentional decision of intelligent, thoughtful, caring, and compassionate people.

Hierarchy of Intentionality: Ethical, Social, and Individual

People in sustainable economies must respect the hierarchy of intentionality, which is related to but different from the hierarchy of sustainability. The highest hierarchal level or plane of intentional decisions is at the level of ethical or moral values. Ethical values reflect an individual or societal understanding or interpretation of the basic principles or laws of nature. Societal ethics or morality thus reflects the principles by which members of a given society consent to be guided or governed *over time*. The second level or plane in the hierarchy is the level of social and political decisions, which are guided by social values. The social values of a society are reflected in the social norms and legal restraints by which its members agree to be governed *at a particular time*. A society cannot be sustained if its social and political values are persistently in conflict with its higher-level ethical or moral values. The third level in the hierarchy is the level at which decisions and actions are left to the discretion of individuals. By their nature, individuals require some degree of self-determination or autonomy. However, an economy cannot be sustained if individual actions are allowed to conflict with the social values or ethical principles by which the people as a whole have consented to be governed and to live.

Higher Levels Define Purpose, Lower Levels Affect Possibilities

As is the case with the hierarchy of sustainability, higher levels of intentionality define the purpose of lower levels and the lower levels define the possibilities of the higher levels. The various levels of intentionality are reflected in various political, legal, and technical institutions and instruments for transforming human intentions into decisions and actions. Constitutions, charters, and other national political documents reflect the ethical principles by which governments are to function. Such documents also define the purposes for which a nation was formed and for which it continues to function—as a nation rather than as individual states, provinces, regions, or districts. Any organization without a purpose has no logical reason to exist and cannot be sustained over time. A nation with no clear common sense of political purpose among its people is not sustainable, regardless of whether it is democratic, socialistic, or autocratic. A common purpose and set of guiding principles are necessary to guide decisions at the next lower level, which is the societal level. Societies rely on a common sense of purposes and principles in establishing their legal structures of laws and regulations to guide both their social and economic relationships. Societies rely on a body of knowledge or technologies to pursue their individual and collective interests within those self-imposed legal bounds.

As with nature, the lower levels of the hierarchy of intentionality affect the possibilities of the higher levels. An inability of people to reach a consensus on matters of purpose and principles severely limits the possibilities of forming and maintaining functional societies and economies. As history has proven, a nation cannot be sustained without the consent of its people, regardless of whether its government is democratic, socialistic, or autocratic. A government that functions with the consent of the governed is *capable* of economic sustainability. The potential of societies depends on the commitment of individuals. The unwillingness of individuals to moderate their self-interests severely limits the possibilities for creating sustainable societies. People within a society must be willing, individually and collectively, to devote the necessary time, energy, and money to establishing and maintain the governing structure of a sustainable society. The possibilities of societies depend on individuals and the possibilities of cultures depend on societies.

Higher Levels Are Slower and More Durable

As with the hierarchy of nature, higher levels of intentionality act more slowly and are more durable than are lower levels. National charters and constitutions require a consensus, whereas laws and regulations require far less public input and less widespread approval. Charters and constitutions reflect deeply held ethical and moral principles, whereas laws and regulations reflect only the means by which those principles are expressed under specific economic and political conditions. Laws that are appropriate at one time may not be appropriate at another. Thus, laws and regulations may need to be changed quickly with relatively little direct involvement of the people. A society's interpretation of its basic ethical and moral principles typically changes only after decades, sometimes centuries. Thus, constitutions and charters tend to be more durable and change less quickly than do laws and regulations.

Likewise, knowledge evolves continually and technology changes continuously. Thus, individuals and businesses routinely and continually change their strategic responses to various laws, rules, and regulations. They tend to search for technologies and strategies that will minimize the effects of restraints on their incomes, profits, and economic growth. Thus, changes in individual behavior may lead to changes in laws and regulations or even changes in social values. However, social and legal structures tend to be more durable and change more slowly than do the knowledge bases and technologies that lead to changes in business strategies and individual lifestyles.

Higher Levels Set Limits

Finally, as suggested previously, higher levels set limits and constraints on lower levels in the hierarchy of intentionality. Societies differ widely in establishing the ethical and social bounds within which decisions are left to the discretion of individuals. Capitalist nations tend to emphasize the importance of individual freedom, whereas socialist nations tend to emphasize individuals' social responsibility. Humans obviously need some measure of autonomy or independence to thrive and become productive members of society. Complete deprivation of personal freedom is considered among the harshest of punishments in virtually all cultures. The debate is likely to continue over how much individuality is too little and how much is too much. Regardless of the form of government, economic sustainability requires that people at the lower level of intentionality recognize and consent to support the essential limits and constraints on individual actions set at higher levels of intentionality.

Alignment of Hierarchies Is Essential for Sustainability

Sustainability does not depend on any particular political process or approach to political decision making. Sustainability only requires that the hierarchy of intentionality be in harmony with the hierarchy of sustainability. The cultures and constitutions that define the principles by which nations function must be in harmony with the ecological, social, and economic principles essential for sustainability. The politically defined laws and regulations enacted and enforced through the processes of government must give priority to the long-run needs of society and nature over the economic preferences of individuals. Individuals must have the autonomy or freedom to use available knowledge and technologies to pursue their individual self-interest, but only to the extent that their economic interests are not in conflict with the long-run well-being of society and nature.

In addition, the decision-making processes of individuals and societies also must be aligned with the hierarchy of sustainability. Decisions involving ethical and moral issues must be made by consensus. Sustainability is ultimately an ethical or moral issue. Current generations have no possible economic or social interests in generations of the distant future. Ethical values are immediate; social and economic values are deferred. A commitment to the future of humanity is an ethical commitment. A consensus cannot make something right that is ethically wrong. There is no way of knowing with certainty what is right or wrong. A consensus is simply the best means available for societies to discover and articulate the purposes and principles by which *they* will define right and wrong. These principles must include the essential principles of sustainability if their economy is to be sustainable. Consensus, though obviously imperfect, is the best means available for discovering such principles.

Decisions involving social issues must be made by collective processes that accommodate the preferences of particular individual societies. Such social decisions are reflected in the social norms, laws, and regulations that are meant to guide and govern the behavior of individuals within society. In democracies, such decisions are made by "the people"; in socialist states, these decisions are made by "the party"; and in autocracies, societal decisions are made by "the ruler." Any of these forms of government could be sustainable, as long as societal decisions are consistent with a consensus of the people, which in turn reflects the essential principles of sustainability. The critical issue is that decisions at the hierarchal level of society are not left to the discretion of individuals. Societal matters require that individuals become involved collectively in a process of decision making, by either initiative or consent.

At the lowest level in the hierarchy of intentionality, individuals are free to make their own independent decisions, without collaboration or consultation. The only condition is that individual decisions must not conflict with the social norms, laws, or regulations established by the society. Thus, the individual level of decision making is aligned with the economic level in the hierarchy of sustainability; the societal level of decision making is aligned with the social level in the hierarchy of sustainability; and the ethical level of decision making is aligned with the level of nature in the hierarchy of sustainability, including the level of human nature. The hierarchy of intentionality is then aligned with the hierarchy of sustainability.

Respect for the hierarchies of sustainability and intentionality are both essential for economic sustainability. The whole of the economy is a part of society and the whole of society is a part of nature. Humans make intentional decisions that affect and are affected by all of the other elements of nature, including other humans. The intentional actions of humans must respect the laws of nature, including the nature of humans, if nature is to sustain humans. Human intentions must function in harmony with the principles of sustainability. Such a view of the world is essential to understanding and achieving economic sustainability.

Study and Discussion Guide for Individual Readers and Group Leaders or Instructors

- Search the Internet or a library for at least two comprehensive definitions of the term "worldview" or "world-view." At least one definition should be from Eastern philosophy and one from Western philosophy.
- Identify at least two current examples of public issues or controversies that relate to the ecological, social, and economic hierarchy of sustainability. The examples should include at one local or national issue and one global issue.
- Identify the significant ethical, social, and individual dimensions of at least one of the previously identified issues or controversies.
- Evaluate the alignment between the hierarchies of sustainability and intentionality for this issue or controversy.

Questions for Individual Reflection or Group Discussion
- What is your definition of *worldview*?
- Do you believe respect for the hierarchy of sustainability is essential to economic sustainability? Why or why not?
- Do you believe purposes and principles are always determined at higher levels of organization? Why or why not?
- Do you believe economic sustainability is essential for social and ecological sustainability? Why or why not?
- Do you believe respect for the hierarchy of intentionality is essential to sustainability? Why or why not?
- Why are your answers to these questions important to the people of your nation, your community, and to you personally?
- After thinking about these questions, what might you do differently to make life better, for others and for yourself?

3

Ecological Principles Essential to Economic Sustainability

Sustainability Is Anthropocentric

Sustainability is inherently an anthropocentric or human-centered concept. The essential questions of economic sustainability are about meeting the needs of *humans* of both present and future generations. Sustainability is also eco-centric, or nature-centered, in that humans are integrally and critically interconnected with the rest of nature. In fact, humans quite likely are the greatest single threat to the sustainability of the rest of life on Earth. If sustainability was about meeting the needs of nature in general, the most logical means for achieving sustainability might be to eliminate the human species. A less drastic possibility would be to depopulate the earth of humans to some easily sustainable level. However, the purpose of sustainability is to sustain both the quality and quantity of human life on Earth, uniquely but certainly not exclusively.

Questions of sustainability are rooted in human philosophy and ethics. Concerns for sustainability arise from the philosophical belief that humanity has some meaningful purpose on Earth that is yet to be fulfilled. That purpose is not clearly definable but is assumed to be morally and ethically right and good. Otherwise, there is no logically defensible reason for humanity to fulfill its purpose. Sustainability assumes that human life on Earth is worth sustaining. Furthermore, sustainability assumes humans are capable of making intentional choices that can affect the future of humanity for either better or worse. Humanity can choose to live sustainably. None of these propositions can be proven; they are accepted as matters of fact by faith. Lacking any one of these essential propositions, human concerns for sustainability would be illogical and irrational. If the human species is not capable of making choices that can fulfill some useful purpose, sustainability is an illogical and irrational concern of humanity.

Returning to the hierarchy of sustainability, humanity is inherently dependent on nature for everything that sustains human life. All living and nonliving things, including humans, are part of the same complex whole of matter and energy. The molecules that make up human bodies are the same molecules that have been on the earth since its beginning, the same molecules that have made up the bodies of all living species of all times. The energy that fuels both human bodies and the electrical impulses perceived as human thoughts is the same energy that permeates the universe and continually transforms everything within it. Everything and everybody in the past was made from this same matter and energy, as will everything and everybody in the future.

Economic sustainability is ultimately dependent on the ability of natural ecosystems to capture and store sufficient quantities of solar energy, particularly biological energy, to sustain human life on Earth, as explained in chapter 1. Humans are capable of capturing and storing solar energy in various forms, but humans rely uniquely on the biological energy captured and stored by the other living and nonliving elements of natural ecosystems. Thus, healthy, productive natural ecosystems are essential for both social and economic sustainability.

Principles of Sustainability Are Laws of Nature

The purpose and principles by which nature functions are determined at the highest hierarchal level, beyond the hierarchy of sustainability, beyond human intervention, observation, or complete understanding. The principles or laws that both empower and restrain human life on Earth are the same principles that define the functions of all other living and nonliving elements of the universe. The laws of science, such as laws of gravity, motion, and energy, are examples of attempts to define the basic principles by which nature functions. Such laws exist, regardless of whether they are understood or accepted in human cultures. If a person drops a heavy object on a fragile surface, the fragile surface will be crushed, no matter how vehemently the person may deny the law of gravity. If energy is used and reused, its usefulness eventually will be lost, even if the users of energy fail to understand or respect the law of entropy.

Living things, by nature, are different from nonliving things in that living things are self-making or regenerative. They rely on solar energy, directly or indirectly, to renew, regenerate, and reorganize their physical structures to accommodate changes in their natural environment. Living organisms also differ from nonliving mechanisms in that living things do not function with the mechanical precision of the nonliving world. The principles of living systems can't be measured in mathematical equations or precise formulas such as those that define mechanical, chemical, and electrical processes. The principles that govern the functions of living systems are no less true or inviolable than those that govern nonliving systems, although they are less well known and appreciated. The laws of nature that define the functioning of living natural systems are commonly known as the principles of ecology.

Holism: An Essential Principle of Ecological Sustainability

The first essential principle of ecological sustainability is *holism*—meaning everything is interconnected. The principle of holism can be summarized by the simple statement, "A whole is more than the sum of its parts." The essence of the whole of any living system—biological, social, or economic—is not fully embodied in its individual parts or members. Wholes have properties that are not present in any of their separate parts but emerge only when the parts come together to form a coherent whole. Parts have properties when they are part of the whole that disappear when the parts are separated or isolated from the whole. The relationships among the parts of wholes matter; when relationships change, the whole is changed.

In situations where interconnections are weak or simple—as in mechanical, chemical, and electrical systems—ignoring holism doesn't appear to be a critical concern. Mechanistic paradigms seem to work very well in matters related to physics, chemistry, engineering, and the industrial arts. The greatest advances during the modern era of science and industry have been in these areas. Where relationships are strong and systems are complex—as in ecological, social, or economic systems—ignoring holism has critical consequences. In these areas of application, mechanical paradigms often have created more problems than they have solved. The most important challenges of economic sustainability are not mechanical or industrial, but instead are ecological, social, and economic. The challenges of economic sustainability are symptoms of dysfunctional or counterproductive relationships among the various living and nonliving elements of nature, society, and the economy.

Ignorance of Holism Has Consequences

Water, air, and soil are polluted with chemical and biological waste because people fail to appreciate the importance of their holistic relationship with nature. The human health consequences of pollution include respiratory problems, cancer, food poisoning, and general poor health as well as the economic costs of health care. Today, fossil energy supplies are dwindling and the polar ice caps are melting because people failed to appreciate the importance of their connectedness with natural ecosystems. The consequences of ecological ignorance are not just violent storms and rising oceans but also a growing realization that today's generations are betraying a sacred trust to keep the planet livable in the future.

The greatest human impacts on nature are indirect, the impacts of economies and societies on nature. When people buy food, they are supporting farmers and food manufacturers and distributors who have specific kinds of impacts on the soil, air, water, and energy. When they buy any material goods—grown, harvested, or manufactured—they are supporting a particular production and distribution process that has specific impacts on natural resources. When they invest in corporations through stock markets, they are supporting companies that have specific kinds of impacts on the natural environment. Economic choices have major impacts on the ecological integrity of natural ecosystems.

The collective public choices of societies may have even greater ecological consequences than do individual choices. These consequences are not limited to the presence or absence of government regulations protecting the natural environment from pollution. Government policies affecting agriculture, manufacturing, labor relations, capital investments, employment, economic growth, all have direct and indirect impacts on the natural environment—locally, nationally, and globally. People have no way of knowing how large or small their individual or collective impacts may be, but understanding of and respect for the ecological principle of holism is essential to economic sustainability.

Diversity: An Essential Principle of Ecological Sustainability

A second essential principle of ecological sustainability is *diversity*. The whole of a thing is said to be diverse if it has a variety of different or dissimilar elements or parts. As one can readily observe, nature is inherently diverse. If nature were not diverse, it would not be capable of reproducing, regenerating, or sustaining life. Entropy is the process of degrading or using up the usefulness of energy and matter, as explained in chapter 1. The ultimate state of entropy is characterized by inert uniformity of component elements—the absence of form, pattern, structure, or differentiation. Barren deserts are capable of supporting relatively little life because they are lacking in ecological diversity. Ecosystems completely lacking in diversity have no useful energy left to support life.

Diversity gives living systems their capacities to renew and regenerate— to live, grow, mature, produce, reproduce, and evolve. Diversity provides the resistance and resilience needed to endure and recover from unexpected threats to health or life, such as physical attacks and diseases. Diversity allows living systems to adapt and evolve to accommodate their ever-changing environment. Even if people do not fully understand the specific nature of a threat, they can readily understand that loss of diversity in general represents a growing threat to the future of human life on Earth.

Ignorance of Diversity Has Consequences

Prior to the spread of humans across the globe, species extinction most certainly occurred, but generally at fairly steady rates. Fossil records indicate that species typically have lasted only about ten million years and only about one in a thousand of all species that ever existed remain on Earth today. The last great mass extinction occurred about sixty-five million years ago, the end of the age of dinosaurs, when some catastrophic event blocked the inflow of solar energy. Since that time, as the human species has spread to each new region of the earth, large mammal species, such as mastodons and mammoths, systematically disappeared.

During the modern industrial era of economic development, which supported rapid growth in human populations, species extinctions have accelerated to rates unprecedented since the age of dinosaurs. During recent decades, species have been becoming extinct at a rate estimated as high as one species every twenty minutes. Some experts estimate that at least half of existing species will be extinct by the end of 2100. This time humans are the global catastrophe. The future of humanity is at risk because too many humans have ignored the essential ecological principle of diversity.

Laws protecting endangered species have generated great public controversy in many countries. Opponents question why people should sacrifice potential jobs and economic well-being to protect rare and economically unimportant endangered species. They fail to understand that the primary motive for protecting endangered species is to protect the future of humanity. Humans are a part of the same global ecosystem as the endangered species. If humans destroy the diversity of the earth's ecosystems, they will also destroy the earth's ability to support human life. There is no way of knowing how many more species can be lost, if any, before the ecological balance is tipped toward extinction of the human species.

Diversity: Best Single Indicator of Ecological Health

Diversity is the single most important indicator of the health of natural ecosystems. The causes of species extinction are too complex and interrelated to develop a strategic plan or detailed legal process for stopping this destructive process. Instead of developing strategies or plans of action, societies must learn to rely on the basic principles of ecosystem health, beginning with the principle of diversity. Single individuals do not have the power to enforce endangered species laws, but they can help others understand the importance of such laws.

The greatest single threat to ecological, social, and economic diversity is the industrial approach of economic development. The industrial strategies of specialization, standardization, and consolidation of control allow societies to extract useful energy from the earth's natural resources more efficiently. However, specialization and standardization destroy the form, pattern, structure, and differentiation necessary for living systems to capture and store solar energy. Industrialization systematically destroys diversity and accelerates the process of entropy.

Species other than humans also specialize, simplify, and establish hierarchal control within natural ecosystems. However, nature sets limits within which individual species must function to maintain the health of their ecosystems. If the species within living systems become overly specialized, they develop complex internal dependencies and eliminate the redundancies that have allowed them to respond to threats and adapt to change. Barring an ecological collapse, a dominant species may emerge and eventually grow in numbers until it kills off the other species, depletes its energy sources, and degenerates into mass starvation or disease. These are nature's ways of dealing with excessive specialization. Humans are not exempt from the laws of nature. Humans have become the dominant species in a highly specialized and incredibly complex global ecosystem. Humans are destroying the biological diversity of the earth and moving the global ecosystem closer to ecological collapse. To stop and then reverse ecological degradation, humanity must respect the principle of diversity. Respect for the ecological principle of diversity is essential for economic sustainability.

Interdependence: An Essential Principle of Ecological Sustainability

A third essential ecological principle of sustainability is *interdependence*. Dependence is exploitative, independence is limiting, but interdependence is mutually beneficial; there are no losers. Interdependence is the reward or pay-off for respecting the principles of holism and diversity. Within interdependent systems, the output of one process becomes input for others. For example, each species in a diverse natural ecosystem provides the food or energy for other species. The wastes of one species provide resources for other species. The flows of matter and energy are circular or recycling rather than linear. The control of natural ecosystems is decentralized or dispersed rather than centralized or consolidated. For example, each different species has a degree of independence, in that it is not dependent on any other specific species but instead is dependent only on the system as a whole. This mutually beneficial nature of interdependent relationships makes the whole of diverse living systems something more than the sums of their parts, rather than something less.

Interdependent relationships involving humans are matters of choice rather than necessity. Previously independent individuals choose relationships that make their lives better. The dependence of people on nature obviously is a matter of necessity rather than choice. However, people have the choice of continuing to exploit and extract from nature, or they can choose to renew and regenerate nature—to work in harmony with nature. Throughout most of human history, humans were far more dependent on nature than was nature on humans. Nature often seemed to deny humans their basic necessities of life. Floods, droughts, pests, and plagues decimated human settlements and destroyed entire societies. Understandably, people throughout history have worked to become less dependent on nature. Unfortunately, the people in many cultures chose to fight against nature rather than work with nature for the mutual benefit of both. The dominant society of today—the modern industrial society—has been very "successful" in its battles with nature. Societies have dammed streams, irrigated fields, poisoned pests, and vaccinated against plagues. But nature has always fought back with bigger floods, longer droughts, more resistant pests, and more complex plagues. If humanity is to survive, people must choose interdependent, mutually beneficial relationships with nature.

Ignorance of Interdependence Has Consequences

After all of the victories of humans over nature, humans still are no less dependent on nature. However, humans are now capable of doing great damage to nature; the well-being of nature has become dependent on humans. Nuclear radiation, acid rain, greenhouse gasses, and other means of mass extermination now threaten the integrity of the biosphere. If humanity chooses to fight to the bitter end, nature will win the last battle—humans can't survive without nature but nature quite likely can survive without humans. Societies can't conquer nature without destroying themselves, but they might do critical damage to nature in the process. Thus, nature also has something to gain from an interdependent relationship with humans. If humanity is to benefit from nature, nature also must benefit from humanity. Humanity must learn to respect the principle of interdependence.

Historically, indigenous cultures have recognized and valued their interdependence with nature. They believed nature was sacred, an earthly manifestation of some higher level, beyond the realm of human understanding. They treated the plants and animals they depended on for food as beings deserving of their respect. They believed animals willingly offered themselves to be killed as purposeful sacrifices. The purpose of those animals was to provide food, just as the purpose of plants was to provide food. Many indigenous societies nurtured the plants and animals, not overhunting or overgathering any species. They left enough to provide food for other plants and animals and for other humans in the future. Indigenous societies that failed to respect their interdependence with nature failed to survive.

Society today shows very little respect for any kind of life other than human life. Much of the meat, milk, and eggs in industrial nations today are produced in giant animal factories, where animals barely have room to move, are fed antibiotics daily to mitigate their inherently unhealthy environment, and suffer the inevitable stresses of caged animals, until they are hauled away and terrorized before being slaughtered. These industrial food systems show no sense of dignity or respect for the lives they propagate, promote, and then destroy. The conditions of life, death, and dismemberment of animals are simply matters of economic efficiency. All forms of life ultimately provide nourishment for other forms of life. However, when humans disrespect and degrade the life that supports their life, they are diminishing the quality of their own lives. Humans must respect their interdependence with nature.

Humanity can continue to take from nature, but humanity also must be willing to give back to nature. People must respect the fact that if they try to take too much too fast, they ultimately will destroy themselves. Humans must not create more waste than nature *can* digest or the kinds of wastes that nature simply *can't* digest. Nature is too complex for humans to manipulate or manage for their own benefit. People can select things from nature that meet their needs, but if they attempt to *redesign* nature to meet their needs, they may unwittingly redesign their own nature. In fact, nature is perfectly designed to meet human needs if humans are willing to respect nature's needs as well. Respect for the ecological principle of interdependence is essential to economic sustainability.

Ecological Principles Apply to Social Relationships

Everything is interconnected. Thus, the principles essential for ecological sustainability are also essential for social sustainability. Families, communities, and societies are more than collections of individuals; they are members of interconnected wholes. Families have properties that are not present in any of their individual members. Whenever relationships within families change, the nature of the family is changed. In reality, families are defined by the fact that relationships *within* families are different from relationships *between* family members and those outside the family.

Communities are groups of people who feel some sense of connectedness and common commitment to the community as a whole. Communities whose members have no shared commitments or shared vision for the future are not really communities but simply collections of individuals. The same holds true of societies that lack a commitment to a common good or common future. To maintain positive relationships, families, communities, and societies must be treated as interdependent wholes.

Diversity adds strength and durability to human relationships by increasing their resilience and regenerative capacity. A diverse group of individuals can share their strengths, come up with different ideas, and find different solutions to problems. From a broader, long-run perspective, diversity among past societies has allowed humanity to survive the decline, fall, and demise of many great civilizations of the past. When one civilization has fallen, there has always been another to arise and carry forward the cause of human progress. Social well-being and human progress are dependent on the principle of diversity.

Interdependence is also an essential aspect of social relationships. The sustainability of social relationships depends on mutually beneficial solutions to problems that inevitably arise among friends and within families and communities. Dependent relationships make families, communities, and other socially connected groups something less; interdependent relationships make them something more. A significant part of that something more is the basic human value of being connected, respected, and esteemed, of belonging, caring and being cared for, loving and being loved. Positive social relationships must be sustained by the principle of interdependence.

Ecological Principles Apply to Economic Relationships

Holism, diversity, and interdependence are also essential in sustainable economic relationships. Economic sustainability requires economic organizations to be managed as wholes rather than as collections of specialized functions, individuals, departments, and divisions. Economic organizations have emergent properties that do not exist in their separate parts. All functions, departments, and divisions must function in harmony if the organization is to function efficiently and effectively. Individuals must decide how to use their abilities and assets to help produce things of value. If there is no reason for individuals, departments, and divisions to work together as a whole, there is no economic advantage in forming or continuing an organization. Sustainable economic organizations must be organized and managed by the principle of holism.

Diversity strengthens economic organizations by allowing them to manage the risks inherent in all potentially profitable ventures. If one division of a diverse organization is unprofitable, profits from another dissimilar division can help offset its losses. Diverse organizations employ people with diverse abilities and talents. If one person can't solve a problem, someone else probably can. Diversity gives economies and other economic organizations the resilience and regenerative capacity necessary for sustainability. Sustainable economic organizations must be organized and managed by the principle of diversity.

Sustainable economic organizations also must be managed by the principle of interdependence. Profits generated through extraction and exploitation simply cannot be sustained over time. Sustainable economic relationships must be mutually beneficial. Both parties to economic transactions must receive more value than they give. In interdependent economic relationships, both trading parties value the things they trade away less than they value the things they receive in return. If individuals or organizations continually exploit and extract, eventually they will run out of resources to extract and people to exploit. Sustainable economic relationships must be built upon the principle of interdependence.

Indigenous societies didn't need to study ecology; they understood ecology because they lived through ecology. The principles of nature were relevant to all aspects of their lives. Until as recently as the mid-twentieth century, nearly three-fourths of the people in the world continued to live and work in proximity to nature in rural farming, fishing, or logging communities. By the early twenty-first century, economic globalization had caused mass migrations from rural to urban areas, which resulted in more than half of all people living in urban areas. With industrial globalization, personal connections with nature have been weakened and, for many, have been lost from social consciousness. Humanity today is suffering the ecological, social, and economic consequences of this lost sense of interconnectedness with nature. To restore economic sustainability, both within nations and globally, people must respect the essential ecological principles of holism, diversity, and interdependence in all aspects of their lives.

Study and Discussion Guide for Individual Readers and Group Leaders or Instructors

- Search the Internet or a library for at least two references to nature or natural ecosystems. At least one reference should view nature as something to be "managed" for the benefit of humans and one should view humanity as a part of nature.
- Identify at least two current examples of public controversies arising from ignorance or disrespect for the essential principles of ecology—holism, diversity, and interdependence. At least one of the examples should be a social or economic issue rather than an ecological issue. Identify the ways in which specific ecological principles relate to this issue.

Questions for Individual Reflection or Group Discussion
- Do you believe sustainability is anthropocentric (human-centered)? Why or why not?
- In what ways are living systems like and different from nonliving systems?
- How would you define an *emergent property*?
- Do you believe diversity is the most important principle of ecology? Why or why not?
- Do you believe nature has an interdependent relationship with humanity? Why or why not?
- Why are your answers to these questions important to the people of your nation, your community, and to you personally?
- After thinking about these questions, what might you do differently to make life better, for others and for yourself?

4

Social Principles Essential to Economic Sustainability

The Significance of Society

Society, as a general concept, includes all direct and indirect relationships among people—within families, friendships, communities, and nations. Humans are interrelated with the whole of nature, but their relationships with other humans are unique and special. Because of their similarity, humans naturally assume other humans have thoughts and feelings like their own. People can't know what it's like to be a dog, a fish, a bird, or any other species, but they know what it's like to be a human. Feelings of self-worth or self-esteem are based in large part on the worth or esteem they feel for other people with characteristics similar to their own. They understand how to treat another person the same as they would like to be treated because they can imagine themselves in the same situation as the other person. They know how to be helpful or hurtful because other people have helped or hurt them. Perhaps most important, they understand that how they treat other people and how other people treat them is important. Because they are human, they know human relationships are important.

Human history verifies the inherent social nature of the human species. Humans instinctively have sought recognition and approval from their fellow human beings. They have banded together in families and communities or tribes, not just for security, trade, and reproduction but also for personal companionship. People need other people to share their joys and to comfort them in their times of sorrow. People need to love and be loved—without rationalization or justification. People need relationships with other people for reasons that are purely personal—not economic.

Some part of an individual's personality may be inherited or passed on genetically. However, the social structures, traditions, and standards of behavior experienced within families and communities are critical to personal development. An independent individual may gain the ability to think, feel, strive, and work. However, societies provide individuals with their specific ways of thinking, with language, information, and insights into how the world works and their place within it. The essence of the individual is shaped by his or her social environment, particularly during early stages of development. The economy is a means of meeting the impersonal, instrumental needs of people as individuals, but positive social relationships are also essential for economic sustainability.

The Uniqueness of Human Society

Humans obviously are not the only social species. Many insects, such as ants and bees, form large communities to share the necessary tasks of survival and reproduction. Many birds, including ducks and geese, migrate and forage in flocks rather than as individuals. Some large animals, such as apes and elephants, live together as extended families. Social patterns among bees, birds, and apes are thought to be determined solely by their genetics or heredity, down to the smallest detail. The social behaviors of nonhuman species are thought to be instinctive. The social behavior of humans, on the other hand, is obviously thoughtful and intentional.

For humans, relationships are not simply a means of survival, security, or reproduction. The unique human capacities for memory, communication, reasoning, and abstraction have allowed the species to expand its horizons and to seek relationships that enhance the quality of human life, rather than just the duration, reproduction, or quantity of life. This uniquely human motive has been readily apparent throughout human history in cultural traditions, social institutions, and civic organizations and in art, music, and literature. The motives for these advances in human society were social, not just economic. Respect for the importance of purely social relationships is essential to economic sustainability.

Social Values and Principles

Social values or norms of human behavior reflect a common understanding of the necessary means for sustaining positive human relationships. As indicated in chapter 1, social values evolve into cultural or ethical values. Cultural values reflect a particular society's understanding of the laws of nature that apply specifically to human relationships. The social values of a particular culture then are attempts to translate nature's principles of positive human relationships into practical guidelines for day-to-day living. Whereas social *values* may be different for different communities and societies at different times in their social evolution, the most fundamental of social *principles* are the same for all communities within all societies at all times. Social principles are a subset of the basic principles or laws of nature, which include the human subset or segment of nature. As with the laws of physics or chemistry, if people misinterpret or intentionally ignore the basic laws of human nature, sooner or later they will suffer the negative consequences.

People in different cultures obviously have different social values, but a common set of core values is shared across virtually all cultures of civilized society. These core values include such human characteristics as *honesty, fairness, responsibility, respect,* and *compassion.* Such values reflect deeper underlying social principles that transcend societies. Social principles, like ecological principles, are defined at a higher level of organization beyond human observation or full understanding. Over time, however, humans have come to share a common sense of what is necessary for positive human relationships. Scientific consensus provides the clearest possible insights into principles of ecological and other physical relationships. Community consensus, a shared sense of what is right and good, provides the clearest possible insights into the principles of human relationships. Positive relationships cannot be maintained among people who are dishonest, unfair, irresponsible, disrespectful, and uncaring. Such propositions do not need to be proven; they are matters of consensus or common sense.

Trust: An Essential Principle of Social Sustainability

Positive personal relationships must be built on *trust.* Trust is a "rule-based" principle of human behavior, meaning it is a universal standard of conduct deemed appropriate for all people under all conditions. Rule-based principles do not consider the consequences of specific actions; good behavior ultimately is assumed to bring good results. The core values of honesty, fairness, and responsibility are all logical aspects of the principle of trust. Such core values are not situational or conditional; they apply to all situations at all times. To maintain positive personal relationships, people need to be consistently and dependably honest and truthful in words and actions. They need to be fair and impartial in their treatment of others, regardless of their race, age, gender, or any of the other particular social groups to which they might belong. They need to do their share of whatever needs to be done and to follow through on their promises or commitments. A violation of any of these requirements is a violation of the principle of trust. To sustain personal relationships, people need to be both trustworthy and willing to trust.

Betrayal of Trust Has Consequences

Whenever people are trustworthy, relationships grow stronger. Whenever trust is betrayed, relationships grow weaker. Economic exploitation eventually destroys trust. In the narrow pursuit of economic self-interests, deception and outright lying in politics and business often become commonplace and even "socially acceptable," but they destroy public trust. People then feel a need to ensure their verbal agreements with written contracts. Married couples may sign prenuptial agreements, in case their marriage vows or verbal promises are betrayed. Discrimination may become commonplace, in spite of laws against it, because it's more economically efficient to condemn whole groups of people than to evaluate people as individuals. Workers may do as little work as they can get by with and think it's foolish for anyone to do anything more. Persistent economic exploitation invariably creates a culture of distrust that in turn destroys the positive social relationships essential for economic sustainability.

To restore economic sustainability, people must reject cultures that foster or promote cynicism, skepticism, and doubt. People must expect and demand honesty from their political and business leaders. They must support politicians who tell the truth and keep promises and reject those who do not, regardless of whether those who lie and cheat might do more for them personally. They must support businesses that are worthy of trust, even if their prices are higher. People probably will continue to need contracts, at least for some matters in complex societies, but people should not expect contracts to sustain good personal relationships. They must take the time to evaluate people on their individual merits and reject discrimination in the workplace and elsewhere. They must accept their share of responsibility, and perhaps even a bit more to make up for the others who don't. To sustain positive relationships, people must be trustworthy and willing to trust others. The social principle of trust is essential for economic sustainability.

Kindness: An Essential Principle of Social Sustainability

Positive social relationships must also be based on *kindness*. The absence of kindness has critical consequences. There are times when relationships can be sustained only through empathy, respect, and compassion. All people face the possibilities of ill health, natural disasters, and financial problems in their lives. All people make mistakes. At times all people need mercy more than they need justice. Kindness is a *care-based* rather than a *rule-based* principle. Kindness is situational, in that appropriate behavior depends on the specific context or conditions under which kindness is expressed. People should do for others as they would have others do for them, if they were in the other person's situation and the other person was in theirs. This ideal of kindness, generally referred to as the Golden Rule, has been a fundamental aspect of virtually every enduring religion and philosophy throughout human history.

Empathy is a precondition for kindness. To be kind, a person first must be able to put him or herself in another's situation, under the other's conditions, with the other's unique obstacles and aspirations. The goodness of an act must be assessed from the perspective of the "person done for" rather than the perspective of "the doer." It's not always kind for a person to treat another person as he or she would like to be treated. The needs, wants, and values of the "person done for" may be very different from those of "the doer." Even though people share a core set of common values, they may have other values that are quite different. People don't necessarily need to agree on everything, but to sustain positive relationships, they must treat others with compassion. At the very least, people must be respectful of the beliefs and values of others.

Lack of Kindness Has Consequences

Trust alone is not sufficient to sustain positive social relationships. To sustain positive social relationships, trustworthy people also must show kindness toward others. People may be completely honest and truthful about their lack of respect and compassion for others. This attitude is often seen among those who honestly and truthfully object to government interference in the free market economy to ensure social equity and justice for the poor and oppressed. They may insist on rewarding people fairly in relation to their contribution to the economy, but are not willing to do anything more. They are open and honest about their belief that poor people are solely responsible for their lack of success. People also can be completely trustworthy but have no respect or tolerance for the values of others. Such relationships are not sustainable. The social principle of kindness is essential to economic sustainability.

True Principles Are Internally Consistent

Ethicists seem to agonize over potential conflicts between core values such as honesty and compassion. However, the truth is revealed through internal consistency. Two truths cannot be in conflict when considered within the context of the larger whole. An untruth won't damage a relationship, as long as it doesn't violate a trust. Friends trust each other not to be hurtful, unless it's necessary to sustain their friendship. If it's necessary, they trust their friends to be truthful, even if it hurts. It's not always unkind to be hurtful.

It is not a violation of trust to discriminate *among* people as long as the discrimination is not *against* people. Respecting real differences among cultures does not violate the principle of trust. It's not necessarily unfair to treat people unequally. It is not irresponsible for people to do less than an equal share when they are incapable of doing more. Respect and compassion for those less fortunate and less capable is not a violation of trust. When in doubt, apparent conflicts among values and principles can be resolved by relying on the necessity for internal consistencies. One truth cannot be in conflict with another truth; one or the other must be untrue.

Courage: An Essential Principle of Social Sustainability

The third essential principle of social sustainability is *courage*. It takes courage to be trustworthy and kind in cynical cultures that consider such values to be idealistic and naïve. It takes courage to act on personal convictions and to persevere in intentions, even in the face of adversity and personal risks. Courage too often is associated with acts of bravery or the willingness and ability to face great personal risks in carrying out commitments. Some of the most evil and despicable acts in the history of humanity were carried out by people with great physical and mental courage. To strengthen human relationships bravery must be guided by social and ethical values. Courage strengthens human relationships only when it gives people the ability to fulfill some positive purpose for the greater good of society and humanity.

There is always a risk that trust will be betrayed. There is always a risk that kindness will be exploited. It takes courage to confront these risks. This doesn't mean people should trust everyone or invest in every potentially worthwhile cause. It doesn't take courage to be careless and reckless. However, people can't allow their fears of betrayal and disappointment to keep them from making worthwhile commitments or carrying through with good intentions. Courageous people must not only act on their convictions, they must also persevere in their actions. Life is not an event; it's an ongoing process. They must find the courage to trust and keep trusting, even when they have doubts. They must find the courage to keep on showing kindness to others, even knowing other people will take advantage of them from time to time. It takes moral courage to sustain social relationships.

Unfortunately, the global economy is dominated by a utilitarian or *ends-based* ethic that places no value on human relationships unless something of economic value is expected in return. The rightness or goodness of decisions and actions is judged solely by their consequences or results, and the economic consequences are the only ones that seem to matter. The supposed objective of such intentions is to do the "greatest good for the greatest number of people." But the "greatest good" has become synonymous with the "greatest wealth," as measured by personal prosperity, regional economic development, or the value of national economic output.

Lack of Courage Has Consequences

People who practice trust and kindness are labeled as naïve for thinking that people can learn to trust each other in the current worlds of business and politics. They are disparaged as idealistic when they express their willingness to pay taxes to support government programs to help the sick, hungry, and poor. They are told that government policies to help the poor create chronic dependencies. They are accused of destroying economic opportunities when they call for policies that protect the natural environment and conserve resources for the future. Both those who are oppressed and those who oppose the oppressing of others are ridiculed if they oppose the conventional economic wisdom that gives economic growth priority over social justice. And when people call for reconciliation, disarmament, and an international rule of law, they are dismissed as utopian idealists. It takes moral courage to speak the truth about the necessity of trusting and caring. It takes courage to be trusting and kind. The social principles of trust, kindness, and courage are all essential in creating the ethical commitment necessary for economic sustainability.

Social Principles Apply to Relationships With Nature

The social principles of trust, kindness, and courage are also essential in defining sustainable relationships with nature. As suggested in chapter 3, some people see the earth as nothing more than minerals, water, air, and energy, as resources to be extracted and exploited for human benefit. Others see the earth as sacred, as something to be worshiped rather than used for any human purpose beyond hunting and gathering. Two true statements cannot be in conflict; one or the other (possibly both) of such statements must be false. If this basic premise is accepted as true, conflicting ecological values can be resolved. The rightness of relationships between humans and nature cannot be in conflict with the principles that define the rightness of relationships among humans.

If people are trustworthy in their relationships with other people, they must be honest, fair, and responsible to others in how they use the resources of nature. If they are honest with themselves, they will realize that their pursuit of individual economic wealth is depleting the natural resource upon which future generations must depend. They will also realize that when they pollute the environment they are threatening the health of people of current and future generations, for the sake of economic efficiency. If they are fair to other people, they won't do things to nature, or condone things done to nature, that diminish other people's quality of life. If they accept their responsibilities for those of future generations, they won't use up the earth's fossil energy unless and until they know there will be enough energy to meet the needs of future generations as well. If people have social and ethical integrity, they will be trustworthy in their relationships with nature.

If people are kind, they will be empathetic, compassionate, and respectful in their use of the things of nature. They will put themselves in the place of those people who lack the economic and political power to protect themselves from exploitation and pollution. They will insist that others be treated as they would like to be treated if they were the ones who lacked the power of self-protection. If they are compassionate, they will be willing to do more than laws and regulations require to protect the environment and to conserve resources for those of the future. They will apply the precautionary principle in ecological decisions, by putting the burden of proof on the potential polluter rather than on those who might suffer from pollution. If they are respectful, they will respect the rights of future generations to an earth as productive and healthy as the world into which they were born. If people have social integrity, they will be kind to other people in their relationships with nature.

Finally, it takes courage to express trust and kindness through relationships with nature. Many people still do not understand, or are unwilling to admit, that their mistreatment of natural ecosystems represents mistreatment of other people. They rationalize that future generations will be capable of finding a substitute for any resource the current generation uses up and of cleaning up any ecological mess the current generation creates. Unfortunately, those who intellectualize and rationalize tend to be those with the greatest economic and political power. They have the power to exact a high economic and political price from those who question or oppose them. In the face of such risks, people must find the courage to be trustworthy and kind to others by protecting nature from economic extraction and exploitation.

Social Principles Apply to Economic Relationships

The social principles of trust, kindness, and courage are equally important in sustaining economic relationships. Such relationships must be based on mutual trust, rather than contracts, rules, and regulations. Legal documents are only useful in dealing with those who are untrustworthy. Even then, contracts can be unfair if they are negotiated between parties with unequal bargaining power, as when one party knows and understands the legal requirements but the other doesn't. In addition, those who are dishonest or irresponsible routinely violate rules and regulations. To them, fines and penalties are just other costs of doing business. Contracts and laws can only force *the few* to conform to the standards of conduct of *the many*. To ensure economic sustainability, *the many* must be trustworthy. Economic relationships can be sustained only if they are based on the principle of trust.

Contrary to popular belief, sustainable economic relationships must also be relationships of kindness. Even if people are trusting in their dealings with others, sometimes trust isn't enough. Sometimes people find themselves in financial difficulties, through no fault of their own, and simply cannot live up to their commitments. If people want to sustain such relationships, they must try to find ways to help others through difficult times and give them a chance to regain their financial footing. Sometimes people need to be willing to make risky loans, pay undeserved premiums or give unjustified discounts, and accept late or reduced payments of financial obligations. Economic relationships can be sustained only through occasional acts of kindness.

Finally, it takes courage to be trusting and kind in economic relationships. Today's world is economically competitive. People are expected to take advantage of every opportunity to get ahead financially, even if it means taking advantage of someone else. Those who trust people they don't know and are committed to acts of kindness are considered naïve and idealistic. However, many are not naïve; they know others will occasionally take advantage of their trust and some will treat their kindness as weakness. They are not idealistic; they know the risks of challenging the conventional economic wisdoms and are willing to take them. To sustain economic relationships, people must find the courage to be trustworthy and kind.

Industrial Development Devalues Social Relationships

Throughout human history, people of all cultures have valued relationships among friends and within families, communities, and societies in general. In fact, culture is a product of human relationships. Relationships were important, not only for individual survival and physical well-being but also for social connectedness and emotional well-being. Industrialization invariably diminishes the value and priority a culture places on social relationships. With industrialization, the priority shifts from relationships as ends, as something that constitutes value in and of itself, to relationships as means to further ends, a way to acquire something of greater value in return. Industrialization is driven by a desire to increase economic efficiency by producing things of ever greater value, not by a desire to make the nature of work itself, including relationships among workers, more enjoyable, fulfilling, or valuable. Relationships are valued for their contribution to the production process, not as end products of immediate value. In the market economies that typically accompany industrialization, relationships that were once largely personal and social are transformed into instrumental, impersonal market transactions.

With industrial globalization, the value placed on social relationships has been diminished still further. The sense of personal connectedness invariably diminishes with distance, making people even less sensitive to the social consequences of economic exploitation. This in turn diminishes or degrades the ethical values of a society. Many contemporary economists deny the existence of ethical values; to them all human relationships are instrumental or a means to some purely economic or personal end. Humanity today is suffering the logical ecological, social, and economic consequences of this lost sense of interconnectedness among people within and among families, communities, and societies. To restore economic sustainability, nationally and globally, people must respect the essential social principles of trust, kindness, and courage in all aspects of their lives.

Study and Discussion Guide for Individual Readers and Group Leaders or Instructors

- Search the Internet or a library for at least two culturally appropriate references to the value of human relationships—within families, communities, or societies. One reference should view relationships as purely economic or instrumental, and one should view relationships as ethical, as an end rather than a means to an end.
- Identify at least two examples of current public issues arising from a failure to respect essential principles of positive relationships—trust, kindness, and courage. At least one of the ex-

amples should be an ecological or economic issue rather than a social issue. Identify the ways in which specific social principles relate to this issue.

Questions for Individual Reflection or Group Discussion

- Do you believe human relationships have purely personal and social value? Why or why not?
- How important do you believe a person's relationships are to his or her personal development?
- Do you agree that essentially everyone believes the core values of honesty, fairness, responsibility, respect, and compassion are essential for positive human relationships?
- How would you explain the difference between a rule-based and a care-based principle?
- How would you define a trusting relationship? Can you sustain an economic relationship without trust? If so, how? If not, why not?
- Does kindness affect your relationship with nature? If so, how? If not, why not?
- How is courage different from bravery? How is courage related to interdependence?
- Why are your answers to these questions important to the people of your nation, your community, and to you personally?
- After thinking about these questions, what might you do differently to make life better, for others and for yourself?

5

Essential Economic Principles of Sustainability

Individuality Is Essential for Sustainability

The fundamental purpose of an economy is to meet the impersonal and instrumental needs of people as individuals. People are capable of contributing to the sustainability of society and humanity only if their economic needs are met as well. These needs include not only tangibles, such as food, clothing, shelter, and health care, but also opportunities for rest, recreation, education, self-actualization, and intellectual growth. Society provides individuals with the potential to produce things of economic value, but individuals must transform this potential into reality. People have the uniquely human capacity to restrain their individual animalistic urges but only if they can meet their basic needs for survival, reproduction, and self-gratification. The economic needs and wants of individuals matter. A society that deprives its members of their economic individuality is not sustainable.

As primitive societies progress beyond self-sufficiency, people turn to barter or trade as a means of further enhancing their individual well-being. They trade with others with the expectation of receiving something of greater individual value in return. With still further progress in individual well-being, people use their economic gains to facilitate more complex means of trade that require some form of currency or money, which facilitates the accumulation of economic surplus. Some of the economic surplus from economies historically has been used to establish and maintain laws, regulations, and communications systems and to support the banks and market infrastructure necessary to facilitate impersonal economic relationships. People in more socially advanced economies have allocated some of their economic surplus to facilitate social relationships and to express their cultural and religious values. However, the pursuit of individual, impersonal self-interest has always been, and remains, the primary motivation for economies.

Principles of Economics Are Principles of Individual Behavior

The essence of economics can be reduced to three basic principles: scarcity, efficiency, and sovereignty. These principles are not the creations of economists; they are basic principles of individual human behavior. These principles exist regardless of whether individuals live in market economies or planned economies. They define the functions people need to carry out to meet their impersonal, instrumental, individual needs. They also define the functions that need to be carried out to pay the economic costs of living in a sustainable society. Few things are more real or relevant to the day-to-day lives of people. People in a sustainable society must respect these essential economic principles of sustainability.

Many people find the discipline of economics to be a confusing, boring, or even depressing field of study. Economics seems too abstract to be relevant to their day-to-day lives. Even if they understand economic theory, it doesn't seem to match their everyday reality. These criticisms are often valid, but they relate far more to the way economics is taught than to economic reality. Despite the complexity of economies and the abstractness of economic theories, the basic principles of economics are quite simple and straightforward.

Scarcity: An Essential Principle of Economic Sustainability

Scarcity is an essential principle of economic sustainability. Things have economic value only if they are scarce—meaning there are not enough for everyone to have all they want. Obviously, the economic value of something is different from its intrinsic human value or its contribution to the greater good of society. For example, air most certainly is valuable to human life but it has no economic value, at least as long as everyone can breathe all they want without sacrificing anything else. Air only becomes economically valuable when it becomes sufficiently polluted or degraded, thus making clean air sufficiently scarce. People then are forced to pay the costs of pollution prevention to get enough clean air. Air then has economic value. Diamonds aren't necessary for human life but they have great economic value. Diamonds are scarce so they command high prices. Intrinsic value is determined by necessity; economic value is determined by scarcity. This may sound simple, but many people don't seem to understand that the economy doesn't necessarily value things that are important to society and humanity.

Scarcity and the Law of Demand

Scarcity doesn't necessarily mean a small amount; it just means not enough to satisfy everyone. For example, most people in the "developed nations" already have more clothes than they need, but clothes still have economic value. Some people are willing to spend money for new clothes rather than wear the clothes they already have. Old clothes are freely available and thus have little economic value, but new clothes are still scarce. The nations of the world with the largest populations typically produce far more food in total than do the nations with the smallest populations. Food is still scarce and thus economically valuable in the more populous nations because there are more people in those nations who need and want food.

As something becomes less scarce, it has less economic value. The economic law of demand is derived directly from this economic truth. The first serving of food at a given meal may taste very good, if a person is hungry. The second serving might taste okay, but by the third or fourth serving, most people will have had more than enough. This is just the nature of humanness. It's a reflection of what is commonly referred to as the law of diminishing returns.

Demand is an economic term or word meaning "willingness and ability to buy." Buyers naturally value more highly things that are scarcer than they value things that are less scarce because of their individual humanness. So sellers can charge higher prices for things when fewer are available for sale but must reduce their prices when they need to sell more of the same things. As a result, prices vary *inversely* with quantity demanded—prices go up, people buy less. This is the essence of the law of demand. The economic law of demand is derived from the economic principle of scarcity.

Scarcity and the Law of Supply

Scarcity also determines the economic value of things offered for sale. To earn money to buy things, people must provide something of economic value to the one who pays them for their work. As people devote more of their time and energy to their work, they have less time and energy left for other activities, including rest and recreation. Their time and energy become more scarce and more valuable as they work longer and harder because they have less time and energy left for their own personal use. Thus, as people expend more time and energy working, they need to be paid more to offset the increasing scarcity of the time and energy left for other uses. So the amount of labor they are willing to supply varies *directly* with their wages or salaries, which is the price of their time and energy.

The situation looks a bit different from the perspective of the employer but the result is much the same. People are likely to become less productive and less valuable to their employers as they work more hours during a given period. Beyond some point, people become physically and mentally tired and, as a result, become less productive. Again, this is a reflection of the "law of diminishing returns" as it applies to the productivity of labor. In addition, workers are unwilling to accept less for their additional work because their free time becomes more scarce and thus more valuable to them. So their employers get less value out of each additional hour of work, and the economic costs of production go up accordingly. The same basic relationship holds for any raw material or resource other than labor used in producing things of economic value, such as steel, chemicals, fuel, or electricity. Producers are willing to produce larger amounts of things only if they can get higher prices to cover their increasing costs of production. Quantities supplied by producers or sellers vary *directly* in relation to prices. This is the essence of the law of supply. Prices go up; sellers offer more for sale. The economic law of supply also is derived from the economic principle of scarcity.

Scarcity and Economic Value

In market economies, prices are determined by the laws of supply and demand. As more of something is produced, the costs of producing it goes up, but its value to buyers goes down, until buyers are willing to pay just enough to cover the costs of production. At this point, buyers would buy more only if prices were lower, but sellers would sell more only if prices were higher. They have arrived at a market price. The most powerful economic concepts are these simple ideas of supply, demand, and market price. Certainly, the real world in which buyers and sellers operate is far more complex than this single product, single market example, but the underlying principles are the same. The global economy has been brought to the verge of collapse by people who failed to understand or respect both the power and the limitation of scarcity and value. People may not like the way the economy values things, or would just rather not think about it, but economic value is determined by scarcity, not necessity.

Obviously, clean air and clean water are more necessary to humanity than are cell phones and sports cars, but the economy doesn't reflect necessity. Women traditionally have been paid less than men in most parts of the world, not because they were less productive but because they were more willing to work in lower-paying jobs. Teachers and nurses are not paid nearly as well as sports stars and movie stars because far fewer people have the physique, talents, and persona to be a "star." People simply cannot expect economic values to protect their air and water from pollution or to distribute income or wealth in relation to human need. The economy values only scarcity. When people understand the economic principle of scarcity, they understand why they must rely on society, not the economy, to value those things that are not yet scarce but still have great intrinsic value to society and the future of humanity.

The principle of scarcity not only determines market values, it is the determining principle of all values that accrue to individuals. Thus, the importance of scarcity is not limited to market economies, which is often overlooked or at least not fully understood. Scarcity would determine the value of various things available to a person even if that person lived a self-sufficient life in isolation from the rest of humanity. Those things that were most scarce in relation to the person's needs and wants would be valued most highly by the individual, and those most abundant in relation to need would be valued least. In planned economies the prices or costs of various goods and services would be set administratively, rather than by markets, but the value of these goods and services to individuals would still be determined by their relative scarcity. Differences between individual values and administered prices in planned economies are often reconciled through barter and other forms of unauthorized trade. The relationship between scarcity and value is a reflection of human individuality. Scarcity is an essential economic principle of sustainability.

Efficiency: An Essential Principle of Economic Sustainability

The principle of efficiency is also essential to economic sustainability. The concept of economic efficiency refers to economic value relative to economic cost. The greater the economic value relative to economic costs, the greater the economic efficiency. The raw materials and human abilities used to produce things of economic value often have a variety of alternative uses. Wood, coal, oil, and natural gas, for example, can be used by a variety of means in manufacturing, generating electricity, transportation, and home heating. Most agricultural land can be used for a variety of crop and livestock enterprises. Many laborers or workers and managers have a wide variety of employable skills and talents and thus a variety of employment opportunities. Economic efficiency is achieved by putting natural and human resources to their highest or best economic use—meaning greatest economic value relative to economic costs.

Economic Efficiency Has Consequences

Profits are linked directly to economic efficiency. The higher the economic value relative to costs, the greater will be the difference between economic costs and returns, which is commonly referred to as profits. Profits can be a powerful motivation for the efficient use of scarce resources. Once natural resources become scarce, profit provides a powerful incentive to reduce resource use, reuse the products made from scarce resources, and recycle waste. Profit also provides increasing incentives to slow the depletion of nonrenewable resources as they become scarcer, thus more economically valuable. Thus, economic efficiency is an important concept in promoting the efficient use of natural resources. However, resource efficiency, while necessary, is not sufficient to ensure economic sustainability. Natural ecosystems may become an unsustainable source of future economic productivity long before natural resources become sufficiently scarce to give these systems adequate economic value to ensure sustainability.

The fundamental purpose of for-profit corporations is to maximize economic returns to their stockholder investments. Profits can be paid out as dividends or invested to enhance the value of corporate stock. Either way, greater economic efficiency means greater economic returns to stockholder investments. This is why corporations continue to exploit natural resources until they become sufficiently valuable to affect corporate profitability. This is also why corporations exploit the resources of society by investing in new technologies that replace workers, rather than employ more workers. Workers demand more wages when their employers make more profits; machines just keep on working. Corporations attempt to set up manufacturing operations in lowest-wage countries for the same reason—greater economic efficiency.

Economic efficiency is also the reason that corporate businesses are reluctant to shift from fossil energy to renewable energy alternatives—fossil energy still produces greater economic value at lower economic costs. Business ignores intrinsic values and costs as they are not economic values or costs. This is also the reason corporations continue to extract and exploit the remaining natural resources in even the remotest places on the earth. The needs of future generations do not affect the scarcity of resources in today's marketplace; they do not affect economic values, costs, or efficiency, so do not affect profitability.

Unlike corporations, individuals can make choices that reflect their social, ethical, and individual economic values. Regardless, people need to allocate their time and money among their various alternative uses as efficiently as possible without compromising their social or ethical values. People quite logically want to get as much value as they can out of the time, energy, or money they have to spend. They need to be efficient. However, a preoccupation with efficiency can cause people unwittingly to compromise their social or ethical values, thus reducing, rather than enhancing, their overall quality of life.

Sovereignty: An Essential Principle of Economic Sustainability

Sovereignty is the first principle of economic sustainability. Returning to the hierarchy of intentionality, sustainability is inherently individualistic as well as social and ecological. The entities that make up human societies and natural ecosystems are distinct and diverse individuals. Sovereignty does not imply complete independence or self-sufficiency; it means being free to choose. People cannot express their individuality fully unless they are free to make their own choices, at least in the areas most critical to their well-being. If people are not free to make economic choices, the economic concepts of scarcity and efficiency are of little consequence, at least to them individually. People must be free to determine or discover their needs and wants for themselves, without force, coercion, or persuasion by others. They must have accurate information so they can know the ultimate value of things before they choose to buy them, not learn later and regret the choices they have made. Sovereign individuals must not be forced, coerced, or even intentionally misled.

Most economists assume that people are sovereign without questioning whether they actually are sovereign. After all, no one is forcing people to buy things. Perhaps people aren't forced to buy anything, but billions of dollars are spent each year on advertising to persuade, coerce, and create social pressures to convince people to buy things they don't need or even want. Many goods and services are advertised and merchandized because they are profitable to those who sell them, not because they are necessary or even useful to the people who buy them. Behavioral psychologists design advertising throughout the global economy today to manipulate the subconscious minds of people, not to facilitate their rational evaluation and choices. Such advertising creates wants that did not previously exist, and then persuades people to strive to meet those wants by spending money for the advertised products and services. Persuasive advertising is destroying economic sovereignty.

Lack of Sovereignty Has Consequences

The global financial crisis of 2008 was a prime example of what happens when credit transactions are based on coercion and deception rather than transparency and honesty. One reason people took out loans they couldn't repay was because lenders were urging them to borrow more money. The lenders knew they could sell these loans to unsuspecting buyers before the borrowers defaulted. Risky loans were "bundled" with safer loans to disguise their lack of value. Others bought homes they never intended to live in because they were told homes were a safe economic investment. Every transaction created a profit opportunity for someone in the financial system. When the deception was revealed, the U.S. housing market collapsed, triggering a global financial collapse.

Many people today are not free to choose how they spend their money because they have been lured into making decisions in the past that have left them with little money to spend on anything else. They owe so much money, they have to use most of their income for debt repayment rather than to meet their current needs. Many others are not free to work where they choose because past decisions have left them with few choices of employment. Many businesses are not free to produce new and better products because they have too much money invested in buildings and equipment that are now obsolete. They are not longer free to choose.

Regardless, individuals who are still free to choose need not sacrifice their economic sovereignty. They can ignore persuasive and coercive advertising and sales tactics. They can buy things that actually meet their needs and satisfy their individual preferences. They can reject the social pressures of the consumerist global society. They can avoid the pitfalls of borrowing too much or becoming too narrowly educated or trained. They can break out of a career path that no longer makes sense—even in their fifties or sixties. They can avoid borrowing so much money for things they think they want that they don't have enough left for the things they know they need. They can refuse to give up their freedom of choice.

People can seek employment outside the corporate mainstream. They can start their own business and produce things they have the ability, or can learn, to produce, for people who share their ethical values. They can break away from corporate or institutional employment and become independent contractors, business consultants, or even start their own schools. Or they can choose to work for people who manage organizations they respect. They can buy things from sovereign individuals and businesses that have chosen to produce the things they need, want, and value. Independent businesses can avoid borrowing so much money that they sacrifice their ability to adapt to changing markets. People can reclaim their economic sovereignty.

Sovereignty in Relations Among Nations

Many individual nations today also suffer from the same basic lack of economic sovereignty. They are being lured into extracting and exploiting their natural and human resources through deceptive promises of economic development that can be used for social and human betterment. They are focusing on production for export to meet the wants of the wealthy rather than production to meet the basic needs of the poor. Their economic sovereignty has been diminished through intentional deception. Many developing countries have been lured into borrowing so much money they have lost their freedom to choose between debt repayment and domestic investments—they struggle even to pay interest on their debts. Their people are trapped in low-skilled, low-paying jobs by a lack of preparation for anything better. Nations, like individuals, must find the courage to break the economic bonds that restrict their sovereignty, by whatever means are necessary. The longer a nation is held in economic bondage, the more difficult it will be to regain its sovereignty. Nations, like individuals, can and must reclaim their economic sovereignty.

For the global economy to function effectively, both individuals and nations must have the freedom to choose how they use their productive resources and how they spend their money, without fear of deception or fraud. These same conditions are necessary for effective individual choices regardless of the type of economy. Self-sufficient individuals or nations isolated from the rest of humanity must be free to choose among whatever resources are available to meet their individual needs most effectively. Individuals and nations that are free to choose may choose to restrict their individual choices for the greater good of society and humanity, for either planned economies or constitutional democracies. Regardless, they must choose freely to restrain their economic self-interests if they are to function effectively. People must be economically sovereign. Although little appreciated among economists, the principle of sovereignty is essential to economic sustainability.

Economic Principles Are Relevant to Relationships With Nature

The principles of value, efficiency, and sovereignty are just as important in managing relationships between people and their natural environment as in managing economic organizations. These are basic principles of individual human behavior. Thus, the ecological value of nature to individuals also is affected by scarcity. However, natural resources often become ecologically scarce long before they are economically scarce and thus become ecologically valuable long before they have economic value. Individual species become more ecologically valuable in sustaining the diversity of natural ecosystems as they become fewer in number or increasingly endangered. The scarcity and value of species and natural ecosystems cannot be measured in dollars and cents, but their relative scarcity is nonetheless important. To sustain a healthy, productive natural environment, people must respect the principle of scarcity in assessing ecological value.

The principle of efficiency also is important in managing or nurturing ecological relationships. The trade-offs of value gained in relation to value sacrificed are as important in ecology as they are in economics. All species compete for space and resources as they attempt to modify their natural environment to accommodate their individual needs. However, humans do so through conscious, purposeful decisions, rather than solely by instinct. Each time humans modify their environment they are sacrificing the potential *long-run* benefits from the species they harvest or displace to gain some *short-run* advantage for themselves. As in economics, at some point the ecological cost of their sacrifice will exceed the ecological benefit they receive in return. In relationships with nature, people must respect the principle of efficiency.

Finally, the principle of sovereignty is just as important in ecological decisions as it is in economic decisions. Natural ecosystems are dynamic—always changing and evolving. Nature is also incredibly complex, with countless interconnections and feedback loops. As a consequence, trends and cycles in natural systems can be explosive or disintegrating. Beyond some point, natural cycles and trends move beyond human influence or control. Thus, if humanity waits too long to correct its ecological errors, it will lose its ability to influence future outcomes. The human species will end up like consumers whose debts are so large they can't make the monthly interest payments, let along reduce their total debt. As humanity pollutes the natural environment, depletes the natural resources of Earth, and alters the earth's climate, the human species is incrementally losing its ecological sovereignty—its ability to choose. Humanity must protect its sovereignty if the species is to have the capacity do the things that must be done now to keep the earth inhabitable for humans in the future. To sustain healthy, productive natural ecosystems, people must respect and protect the principle of sovereignty.

Economic Principles Are Relevant to Social Relationships

The principles of value, efficiency, and sovereignty are essential also in maintaining positive social relationships within families, communities, and societies. The value of interpersonal relationships is affected by scarcity. People may not like to admit it, but the value of additional friendships is inversely related to the number of friends they already have. If a person doesn't have a friend in the world, finding one may be his or her highest priority. If a person has a dozen friends, each may still be valuable, but one more or less won't make nearly as much difference as if he or she only had a couple. Social value is not monetary but is nonetheless related to scarcity. The same holds for families, communities, and cities. The greater the number of people involved, the weaker will be the sense of connectedness and less valuable will be their social relationships. To sustain positive interpersonal relationships, people must respect the principle of scarcity.

Efficiency is also important in maintaining interpersonal relationships. Relationships require time and energy. The time and energy spent on one relationship is not available to spend on another, and the time spent on relationships in total is not available to spend on anything else individuals might do instead. So every relationship has a cost, and the cost can be expressed in terms of the value forgone by not spending time and energy on something else. People get the most out of their interpersonal relationships when they allocate their time and energy among friends, family, neighbors, and society to get the greatest benefit in relation to whatever else they must forgo. True principles cannot conflict; trust and kindness among friends and associates need not be sacrificed for the sake of efficiency. However, people must respect the principle of efficiency in sustaining positive interpersonal relationships.

Finally, sovereignty is as important in sustaining interpersonal relationships as it is in economic relationships. Interdependent relationships among people must be relationships of choice. If one person is dependent on the other, the relationship is inherently exploitive. Even if the dominant person doesn't exercise his or her opportunity to exploit, the dependent person always feels vulnerable and insecure. When people within a society are not free to choose their own form and structure of government, or at least to reject governments chosen for them, they inevitably feel oppressed and exploited, even if they are governed by the most benign of rulers. Friends remain true friends only if each feels free to end the friendship. Neighbors remain good neighbors only if they feel free to be good neighbors with others instead. And people feel a sense of belonging only within societies where they feel free to choose their own destiny. To sustain positive interpersonal relationships, people must respect the principle of sovereignty.

The challenges confronting the global economy today have arisen from ignoring some basic economic principles, such as sovereignty, and distorting and abusing other economic principles, such as efficiency and scarcity. Today's global economies are not made up of sovereign individuals or economic organizations but instead are dominated by large global corporations. People are also being misled, perhaps intentionally, into believing that economic efficiency is somehow equivalent to societal well-being, which suggests that economic value is equivalent to societal value. Many individuals ignore or reject the basic principles of economics because they see no relevance of economics to social or ecological relationships. In cases where economic principles are accurately interpreted and applied, economic values too often are given priority over social and ethical values. The hierarchy of sustainability has been inverted, placing the economy above society and nature. Accurate interpretation and application of basic economic principles are essential to economic sustainability. A sustainable economy must respect the principles of scarcity, efficiency, and sovereignty.

Study and Discussion Guide for Individual Readers and Group Leaders or Instructors

- Search the Internet or a library for at least two culturally appropriate references to the current global economic situation. At least one reference should focus on the economic aspects of the current situation and one should focus on the social and ecological consequences.
- Identify at least two examples of current public issues arising from a failure to respect essential economic principles of scarcity, efficiency, and sovereignty. At least one of the examples should be a social or ecological issue rather than an economic issue. Identify the ways in which specific economic principles relate to this issue.

Questions for Individual Reflection or Group Discussion
- Do you believe that individual independence, freedom, or sovereignty is essential to sustainability? Why or why not? If yes, how much sovereignty is enough?
- How would you define or explain the difference between economic value and intrinsic value?

- How would you explain the "law of diminishing returns" with respect to quantity demanded by buyers? With respect to quantity supplied by sellers?
- How do you relate economic efficiency to profits? To opportunity costs?
- What do you think are the most important violations of consumer sovereignty?
- Do you think it's appropriate to apply economic principles to social relationships? To ecological relationships? Why or why not?
- Why are your answers to these questions important to the people of your nation, your community, and to you personally?
- After thinking about these questions, what might you do differently to make life better, for others and for yourself?

6

Essential Characteristics
of Sustainable Economies

Economies Are Living Systems

The economy is a part of society and nature, both of which are living systems. An economy then is a living system as well—a living organization. Sustainable economies must be designed, organized, and function as living systems, in accordance with the basic paradigm or model of interconnected living organisms. The sustainability of life on Earth ultimately depends on the daily inflow of solar energy, as explained in chapter 1. Only living organisms are capable of capturing, organizing, concentrating, and storing solar energy in the diverse forms necessary to support biological life on Earth, including human life. Unlike nonliving systems, the natural tendency of living systems is to use solar energy to move away from entropy, toward greater diversity of structure, form, hierarchy, and pattern. Only living systems are capable of offsetting the inevitable degradation of usefulness of energy associated with all useful human activities, including all economic activities.

Characteristics of Living and Nonliving Systems

All systems, both living and nonliving, are characterized by pattern, structure, and process. The pattern of a nonliving system is its organizational concept—the plan or blueprint by which it is constructed. The pattern of a living system is encoded in its DNA—the genetic code that guides its developmental processes. The structures of both living and nonliving systems are the physical embodiments of their respective patterns. Structure is the tangible or material aspect of all systems, including all organisms and organizations. Structure can be seen, felt, touched, or otherwise physically perceived, as a plant or animal, a machine or building. Process is the means by which a system performs the necessary functions to fulfill its purpose—the means by which it lives, works, or operates. The processes of both living and nonliving systems are capable of performing useful functions, of doing *work*.

The primary difference between living and nonliving systems relates to the processes by which their physical structures are made or constructed. Nonliving systems must be constructed according to prepared plans or blueprints, but living systems are self-constructed or self-made according to their own DNA. Once built, the structure of a nonliving system remains constant or fixed. The system may break and eventually wear out, but the basic nature of its structure remains unchanged. Nonliving structures can be remodeled, rebuilt, or even redesigned, but they cannot redesign, rebuild, or remodel themselves. Living organisms, on the other hand, are not built or rebuilt, made or remade. Instead, living systems make and remake their own structures, according to their genetic code. The structure of living systems also evolves autonomously from generation to generation. Living systems continually redesign and reorganize themselves. It is the basic nature of living things to make, remake, and reorganize themselves.

Consequently, living organisms are always changing. They are born, mature, reproduce, grow old, and eventually die. There is little physical resemblance between a newborn baby, a healthy mature adult, and a frail old person nearing death. Their physical structure is continually changing, although their genetic pattern remains the same. The cells of living organisms are being replaced continuously, even in mature organisms, creating essentially new structures, often many times during a single life span. When a living organism dies, it becomes a "self-made" nonliving structure; it loses its capacity for renewal. While the pattern of a specific living organism remains unchanged, species of organisms are capable of evolving genetically, from generation to generation, to accommodate their ever-changing environment. Living and nonliving systems may both perform useful functions or work, but a significant proportion of the energy expended by any living system is devoted to the process of renewal and regeneration.

Living Economies Are Holistic

Contemporary or modern economies are designed, organized, and function as nonliving, mechanistic systems. Modern science views the world as a large, complex machine or mechanism. As with other sciences, the science of economics is reductionist. It attempts to examine various parts of the economy in isolation to gain insights into the economy as a whole. For example, the most fundamental concepts of neoclassical economics are rooted in the assumption of *ceteris paribus*—meaning all other things are assumed to be equal or unchanged. The economic laws of supply and demand assume that all things other than quantities and prices are constant. Living systems, however, are holistic—everything is interconnected, and wholes have emergent properties that are not present in their parts. Whenever a component or part of the economy is separated from the economy as a whole, the system loses emergent properties that may be critical to the functioning of the economy. Economic *ceteris paribus* conditions never actually exist because economies are holistic, living systems. The effect of every cause becomes the cause of another effect, in an unending feedback process. Even the simple acts of observation and experimentation can change the context, and thus change the nature of relationships within living systems. Economic sustainability requires a holistic approach to economic inquiry.

Living Economies Are Dynamic

Living systems are inherently dynamic. Economists have attempted to develop dynamic economic models, but economic theory remains rooted in paradigms of "comparative statics," or economic snapshots, rather than true economic dynamics. Econometrics is a popular branch of economics that expresses economic relationships in mathematical formulas and uses statistical methods to estimate the nature of economic relationships. Statistical analysis allows economists to address the variability in economic data used to test hypothesized economic relationships. However, statistical analysis is rooted in the assumption that the structure of systems remains constant—at least long enough to identify and quantify structural relationships. However, the structures of living systems are continually changing, even in the absence of influence or interference from outside the systems. Thus, statistical conclusions, even when relevant to some observed economic structure of the past, may have little relevance to economic structures of either the present or the future within which the results of economic research are applied. As a consequence, economic forecast models are notoriously, sometimes disastrously, inaccurate.

Living Economies Are Individualistic

Contemporary economics is a search for general laws, or specific cause-effect relationships, that are true for all situations. However, living systems are inherently individualistic. Economists attempt to generalize about specific individuals and economic groups, using conclusions drawn from observing other individuals and groups. They attempt to anticipate future trends in one economy based on systematic observations of other economies. However, living systems are unique. No two living organisms are identical, even if they have identical DNA. Unique reactions to unique life experiences cause each individual to be different from any other living individual. Furthermore, each group of living individuals is different from any other group of individuals. The uniqueness of both individuals and individual relationships makes each society and each economy a unique whole. Relationships within one economy will never be the same as relationships within another economy, even if everything else is identical. Thus, economic generalizations are inherently limited in scope, restricted in nature, and, more typical, lacking in credibility.

Obviously, contemporary economic thought has facilitated the creation of many material benefits for humanity during the industrial era of economic development. But the benefits of industrial development have come largely from resource extraction and exploitation, rather than from sustainable productivity. Extraction and exploitation may be appropriate means of mining nonliving natural resources, but they are not sustainable means for managing the living resources of either nature or society. Most of the major ecological and social problems confronting human society today are direct consequences of using nonliving paradigms of economic development to guide the actions of humans within living economies, societies, and ecosystems. Environmental and ecological degradation are direct consequences of the extraction of natural resources motivated by individual, impersonal economic incentives. Social and moral decay, likewise, are direct consequences of the impersonal exploitation of the weak by the powerful, motivated by individual economic incentives. Living organisms and organizations are not like machines or factories; their exploitation has inevitable ethical, social, and, ultimately, economic consequences.

Living Economies Are Purposeful

A sustainable economy must be organized as a healthy living system or organization. All organizations—living and nonliving—must have a purpose. To "organize" means to put together into an orderly, functional structure; to arrange in a coherent fashion; or to arrange for harmonious or coordinated action. An economy is an orderly, functional arrangement of resources, and thus is an organization. Lacking a coherent purpose, there is no logical reason for arranging facilities, finances, and people in any particular way rather than simply allowing them to function independently without order, coherence, or coordination. The purpose of an organization always suggests an appropriate structure and an appropriate set of principles by which the organization should function. An economy is a *purposeful* organization.

Economies, in general, allow people to move beyond self-sufficiency by facilitating specialization or division of labor—individually, temporally, and geographically. However, the purpose of any specific economy must be defined further by the society of which the particular economy is a part and thus is meant to serve. Preferences for particular economic structures and processes—corporations, cooperatives, banks, markets, forms of currency—should not be allowed to determine the purpose of an economy. Instead, economic structures and processes should be designed, and redesigned as necessary, to fulfill the societal determined purpose for an economy.

The purposes of nonliving organizations, such as machines and factories, can be designed into their structure. The various components of the structure can be constructed and arranged in such ways that the purpose of the organization will be achieved if it functions according to its structural pattern or plan. For example, if an automobile is appropriately designed, assembled, and provided with fuel, it will start, run, and take the driver wherever the car has been designed to go. As long as its mechanical structure remains intact, the car will fulfill its purpose. Its purpose is built into its structure.

Living Economies Are Guided by Principles

The purposes of living organizations, however, must be encoded into their operational principles, much as the purposes of living organisms are encoded in their DNA. For example, the structure of a sustainable economy must allow it to be self-making and dynamic, as its structure continually renews, regenerates, and evolves. The genetic code of a living plant or animal includes all of the information needed for the organism to germinate or to be born, to renew its cells, to grow, mature, reproduce, and reorganize as it evolves. The guiding principles of a sustainable economy must include all of the information needed for the economy to meet the needs of the present—the needs of the society by which it was created—without diminishing opportunities for the future of either its own society or humanity. A sustainable economy must be conceived, born, grow, mature, reproduce, and continually evolve, without losing its basic "sense of purpose."

Healthy living systems must continually balance a natural tendency toward greater efficiency with their need for long-run sustainability. The quest for efficiency appears to be a natural characteristic of all living systems. However, in striving for greater efficiency, living ecosystems may become vulnerable to disruption, impairment, and eventual collapse. Even as they evolve toward greater efficiency, *healthy* living systems continue to function by the principles of holism, diversity, and interdependence. They continually reorganize and rearrange their component parts in ways that *reduce, reuse,* and *recycle* the energy that flows through their systems and fuels their productive and regenerative processes. They rely on mutually beneficial relationships among their diverse elements to increase the efficiency of energy use, resulting in greater biological activity or productivity, while slowing the degradation of energy and reducing the rate of entropy.

Three Rs of Economic Sustainability

The so-called "three Rs" of ecological, efficiency, or resourcefulness—reduce, reuse, recycle—while necessary, are not sufficient to ensure ecological sustainability. Since the usefulness of all energy is eventually depleted through entropy, sustainable living systems must also be *regenerative,* as well as efficient or resourceful. Regeneration is an essential aspect of sustainability: in fact, the only means of offsetting entropy. Regenerative systems must rely on solar energy to continually *renew, reproduce,* and *reorganize.* Green leaves and algae are nature's self-renewing biological solar energy collectors. Living organisms also have an innate tendency to reproduce. By their basic nature, plants devote a significant portion of their life's energy to producing seeds and shoots and other means of reproduction. By nature, animals often devote a large portion of their energy to conceiving, gestating, and raising their offspring. By nature, plants and animals redesign and reorganize their structures as they evolve from generation to generation. Sustainable living systems must balance the three Rs of ecological *resourcefulness* with the three Rs of ecological *regeneration*—renewal, reproduction, and reorganization.

In striving to balance efficiency and regenerative capacity, living systems can become vulnerable to disruptions, physical impairments, and potential ecological collapse. Natural ecosystems tend to evolve toward greater complexity and connectivity in their quest for greater efficiency. They gain efficiencies through more narrowly defined specialization of more closely coordinated and increasingly complex interconnections of their functional processes. At some point in the quest for greater efficiency, such systems lose their *resilience* or their ability to withstand or recover from unexpected adversity.

Increasing complexity and connectivity leads to loss of authentic diversity and interdependence. Diverse systems are *resistant*; complex systems are fragile and vulnerable. Systems that are diverse and interdependent are *responsive*; closely connected systems are internally dependent and inflexible. Such systems lack the ability to survive major disruptions. Damage to any part of their system quickly spreads through the system, disrupting and damaging the system as a whole. In the quest for efficiency, systems remove *redundancies* both within and among their various functions. Redundancy is essential to diversity. Efficiency diminishes the ability of systems to regroup or recover from major disruption and impairments; they become vulnerable to collapse. Sustainable systems must balance the three Rs of ecological *resourcefulness* and the three Rs of ecological *regeneration* and the three Rs of ecological *resilience*—resistance, responsiveness, and redundancy.

Balancing Resourcefulness, Resilience, and Regeneration

Natural ecosystems, being self-making and self-regulating, are capable of balancing their need for efficiency with their need for resilience and regeneration. If natural ecosystems fail to maintain a healthy balance among the three essential characteristics eventually they will collapse. They deplete their food supply and starve, die off from disease or conflict, or fail to survive an ecological disruption. Economies, on the other hand, are created and regulated by people who make purposeful choices that affect their efficiency, resilience, and regenerative capacity. In the pursuit of greater economic efficiency, today's global economy is becoming increasingly vulnerable to collapse, through either depletion of its natural and human resources or its inability to withstand major ecological or social disruptions, whichever occurs first.

Managing Sustainable Organizations

The essential characteristics of sustainable economies are also essential characteristics of all types of sustainable organizations, for-profit and nonprofit, and of sustainable ways of life or lifestyles. A sustainable organization is analogous to a living organism and must function as a healthy living system. An individual human is a living organism, and a sustainable lifestyle must reflect the essential characteristics of healthy living systems. Sustainable organizations and individuals are microcosms of economies and must possess the same characteristics as sustainable economies if they are to function sustainably.

Most contemporary sustainability initiatives—individual, public, non-profit, and for-profit—focus on the three Rs of ecological efficiency or resource-fulness. They attempt to *reduce* pollution and energy use; *reuse* materials and products; and *recycle* biological, chemical, and material wastes. All of these strategies improve the efficiency of energy use, since all materials are concentrated forms of energy, wastes are unused energy, and pollution requires energy to mitigate. Since these strategies increase efficiency, they are frequently cost effective or profitable as well as more ecologically sustainable. In other cases, modest government incentives may be sufficient to make such strategies economically as well as ecologically efficient. Quite logically, most government and private sector sustainability initiatives focus on the three Rs of ecological resourcefulness.

Other sustainability initiatives take a first step toward ecological regeneration by substituting renewable for nonrenewable energy resources. By one means or another, they substitute solar energy for fossil energy, as solar energy is the ultimate source of all renewable materials as well as renewable energy. In some cases, as with hydroelectric generation, renewable energy may be economically competitive with fossil energy. In other cases, government programs to protect the environment from pollution reduce or eliminate any economic advantage of using fossil energy. Nuclear-powered generation of electricity is an obvious example. In cases of renewable energy production using passive solar collectors, windmills, photovoltaic cells, and various forms of bioenergy, significant government incentives are required to make renewable energy economically competitive with fossil energy.

Necessary and Sufficient Conditions for Sustainability

Initiatives that focus on reducing, reusing, recycling, or even renewing energy, while logical approaches to resource efficiency and regeneration, can actually become obstacles to economic sustainability. Such strategies can be designed and implemented without rethinking the conventional economic paradigm and without radically redesigning the institutions or organizations involved in the processes. Such initiatives, while potentially beneficial, do not ensure regeneration or resilience and thus do not ensure sustainability. By focusing on the three Rs of ecological efficiency or resourcefulness, an economy may become even less resilient and thus less sustainable. While focusing on renewable energy ensures a regenerative source of energy, it does not ensure that a society's overall capacity for energy regeneration will be sustained. It does not ensure the regeneration of the "social energy" necessary to sustain the productive capacity of society.

Energy efficiency and regeneration depend on the capacity of both nature and society to make solar energy useful in supporting human life. Water impoundments, windmills, and photovoltaic cells are products of the intellect and organization of human societies as well as the physical materials of nature from which the regenerative structures are built. Humans are biological beings and inherently dependent on biological sources of energy, which depend on essential elements of the earth, including clean air, water, and soil functioning together in healthy living ecosystems. Barren deserts provide compelling examples of natural systems that receive abundant solar energy but still support very little life. Reliance on solar energy is necessary but is not sufficient to ensure sustainability.

Equally important, a society that is guided by economic value, whether derived from markets or government subsidies, is fundamentally incapable of sustaining the positive social relationships necessary for sustainability. As indicated in chapter 5, economic value is determined by scarcity, not by necessity. Scarcity means there is not enough of something for everyone to have all they want. Thus, some must receive less than they want. Others invariably receive less than they need for an acceptable quality of life and others even less than they need to survive. By its very nature, a society guided by economic value will leave some people without adequate food, clothing, or shelter—or force some to settle for cheap, unhealthful foods, unsafe shelter, and clothes that won't keep out the cold. Today's global society provides a compelling example of the lack of social responsibility in an economy driven by economic values. A global society in which some prosper while others live in poverty or starve is inherently unstable and unsustainable, even if it relies solely on renewable solar energy. Sustainability ultimately will require radical rethinking, redesign, and reorganization of economies to reflect the paradigm or model of healthy living systems.

Economic Sustainability Will Require Radical Redesign

In summary, as economic organizations and institutions move toward ever-greater efficiency, they eventually compromise the regenerative capacity that is essential for sustainability. As investments become more narrowly focused on economic returns, societies fail to make the long-term investments in natural and human resources necessary for renewal and reproduction of natural and human resources. Such investments cannot compete economically. Societies that are preoccupied with economic efficiency are unwilling to pay the higher costs of sustainability, either in the marketplace or through public policies.

Such societies lack the capacity to radically redesign and reorganize their economy for the benefit of future generations of citizens or investors. Their institutions and organizations may be productive and profitable, but they are not sustainable. To ensure sustainability, they must balance the need for economic efficiency with the need for ecological and social integrity.

In addition, as economic organizations focus more narrowly on economic efficiency, they also compromise the level of resilience that is essential for sustainability. Their functions become more highly specialized and more tightly synchronized and redundancies are systematically removed. In the process, critical dependencies are created among the specialized functions and the systems as a whole become more fragile and vulnerable. They lose their ability to either withstand or respond to unexpected shocks, and their lack of redundancy leaves them without the resiliency needed to regroup and bounce back. If any component of such a system fails to perform its function effectively, the entire system is vulnerable to collapse. Such systems can be highly efficient, but they lack the resistance, resilience, and redundancy needed for sustainability. Reducing, reusing, and recycling are necessary for resourcefulness and economic efficiency but not sufficient for sustainability. Sustainable economics must also be resistant, responsive, and redundant and renewing, reproductive, and reorganizing. The need for economic efficiency must be balanced with the need for ecological, social, and economic integrity.

Authentic Sustainability: New Worldview, New Thinking

Authentic sustainability will require a new understanding of how the world functions and of the capacities of humans to function in harmony with nature. It will also require new ways of learning and thinking to accommodate this new understanding. The new ways of learning and thinking must mimic those of efficient, resilient, regenerative, and thus *complex* living systems. Complex living systems have selective boundaries that are neither closed nor completely open but are selectively permeable or semipermeable. Relationships within a complex system are nonlinear and are affected by continuous feedback loops that can create reoccurring patterns of acceleration, decay, and oscillation. Complex living systems are self-organizing; they have memory and emergent behaviors that are not characteristic of the parts but arise from relationships within the whole. Complex systems are chaotic and unpredictable, but they have the capacity to learn, function, and evolve with purpose. These new ways of thinking about complex systems are typically referred to as *systems thinking*.

New ways of learning must accommodate these new ways of thinking about complex living systems. Collaborative learning, or co-learning, is an essential means of stimulating and cultivating the new ways of thinking necessary for sustainability. In collaborative learning, some are conveners and others are participants, but there are no teachers or students; all are colearners. Collaborative learning goes beyond "groupthink," where groups try to minimize conflict and reach consensus without critically testing, analyzing, and evaluating ideas. It fosters "group intelligence" by creating a culture of openness and the sharing of ideas.

Collaborative learning encourages self-organization and the constructive flow of knowledge and ideas both within and with those outside of the collaborative. It creates and augments intelligence, involvement, imagination, integration, and intuition. It supports and promotes relationships of trust and kindness, humanity, and harmony. It honors collective intuition, supports collective action, and creates a community of abundance where people feel free to share their intellectual, emotional, and spiritual gifts or assets in a collaborative process. It is fundamentally different from traditional paradigms of education. Collaborative learning is essential in understanding economic sustainability as an emergent property of healthy, living systems that function in harmony with the ecological, social, and economic principles of sustainability.

In summary, the essential characteristics of sustainable economies are the characteristics of healthy living systems. Sustainable economies must be self-making, individualistic, and dynamic. Understanding and managing sustainable economies will require new and fundamentally different ways of thinking and learning. Sustainable economies must be managed to achieve balance and harmony among their needs for efficiency, resilience, and regenerative capacity if they are to meet the needs of the present without compromising opportunities for the future.

Study and Discussion Guide for Individual Readers and Group Leaders or Instructors

- Search the Internet or a library for at least two organizations that claim to be committed to sustainability, at least one a for-profit businesses and another a nonprofit organization. Examine their mission statements or guiding principles for statements of commitment to the essential characteristics of sustainable economic organizations.

- Identify at least two examples of current public issues arising from a failure to recognize the essential characteristics of sustainable economies.
- Examine your personal lifestyle and assess how effectively it conforms to the characteristics of a sustainable economic organization.

Questions for Individual Reflection or Group Discussion

- Do you believe sustainable economies must function in the same ways as healthy living systems? Why or why not?
- What do you think are the most important differences between living and nonliving systems?
- In your opinion, what are the most important risks of focusing sustainability initiatives on the three Rs of ecological efficiency?
- Do you believe a solar-powered economy is inherently sustainable? If not, why not?
- Why do you think resilience is so often overlooked and underappreciated in discussions of economic sustainability?
- How would you define *collaborative learning*? How is it different from traditional education?
- Why are your answers to these questions important to the people of your nation, your community, and to you personally?
- After thinking about these questions, what might you do differently to make life better, for others and for yourself?

7

Essential Characteristics of Markets in Sustainable Economies

All Economies Are Mixed: Market and Planned

Virtually all nations of the world have mixed economies, with characteristics of both market and planned economies. In a *pure* market economy, the use of natural and human resources would be allocated among alternative uses entirely by decisions made by individuals participating in competitive markets. Prices would be determined by market competition, and the role of government would be limited to maintaining market competition and facilitating trade. In a *pure* planned economy, the use of resources would be allocated among alternative uses by collective decisions made within various planning agencies of governments. The government also would be responsible for determining the prices for goods and services exchanged among individuals. In practice, all governments incorporate some aspects of both market and planned economies in attempting to serve both the individual and societal interests of their constituencies.

In so-called "market economies," governments use a variety of taxes, subsidies, mandates, and regulations to modify the impacts of markets on the allocation of natural and human resources. Most people understand, intuitively if not explicitly, that even the most efficient of free markets do not serve the common or public interest of a society. In so-called "planned economies," unofficial markets invariably emerge to meet the needs of individuals that are not met through central planning. Governments in planned economies tolerate and often encourage such markets. Most people seem to understand that the individual needs of multitudes of people are simply too diverse to be fully anticipated and met through central planning. Market economies merely rely more on markets and less on government, while planned econo-mies rely more on governments and less on markets. It is critical for those in both market and planned economies to understand the essential characteris-tics of markets and functions of governments that are necessary for ensuring economic sustainability.

Markets Facilitate Choices

The basic function of markets is to provide a convenient means by which con-sumers and producers can make choices among economic alternatives. Choices are a natural consequence of the availability of alternatives or substitutes. In many cases, more than one good or service will serve the same basic economic need or satisfy the same basic preference. Consumers may have many logical and reasonable alternatives from which to choose those that best suit their preferences. Their choices obviously will be affected by the relative prices of the various alternatives. A rise in price of one alternative will cause some buyers to choose another. The better the substitutes, the greater will be the change in quantities of one alternative purchased or chosen in response to a change in the price of another.

As mentioned in chapter 5, some production resources also are more or less interchangeable. For example, different soil types may be equally suited to produce a given crop, and different workers may be equally productive on a manufacturing assembly line. In these cases, alternative resources are equally suited to produce the same basic products. In other cases, different fields, work-ers, or managers can make significant differences in productivity. Quantities of specific natural and human resources used are more responsive to changes in prices or wages when resources have better substitutes in producing the same basic products. In some cases, different combinations of resources—land, labor, management, and capital—can be used to produce the same basic product. For example, mechanization (which requires capital) can often be substituted for labor in producing a given product. Better managers may also be able to produce more output while using the same or even less land, labor, and capi-tal. The quantities of different types of resources used will reflect their relative productivity but also will change in response to changes in their relative prices.

However, the capacity to substitute human and natural resources with other such resources is always limited. Things of economic value are not freely available from nature; they are scarce. Thus, labor and technical know-how must be applied to land or other raw materials to create things of economic value. Humans cannot produce things of *economic* value without natural resources, and natural resources have no *economic* value without applying human resources. Thus, natural and human resources are not infinitely substitutable; both are necessary and neither alone is sufficient. Natural and human resources may be substitutes over some range of use, but natural and human resources ultimately are complements rather than substitutes, in that both are essential for economic productivity. Regardless, a basic function of markets is to facilitate choices among alternatives.

Market Values Are Affected by Individuality, Form, Place, and Time

Markets can provide an efficient and effective means of establishing economic value. However, market values are not a comprehensive or complete measure of values. Market values reflect scarcity, not intrinsic value or human necessity, as explained in chapter 6. Economic value is individual, instrumental, and impersonal. Scarcity depends on how much of something sellers are willing to make available in relation to how much buyers are willing and able to buy. The scarcity and thus economic value of a particular good or service depends on the answers to four basic questions: What is it? Where is it? When is it available? Who is involved in the transaction? The economic value of anything depends on form, place, time, and individuality or possession.

By nature, different people have different tastes and preferences. Thus, different individuals may perceive the value of a good or service differently, even for the same product or service at the same place and time. Economic value is still nonetheless impersonal because the economy is indifferent regarding the specific person who values something more or less than someone else. In such cases, economic value is increased, or new value is created, when a person who values a good or service less exchanges it with or sells it to a person who values it more. Both buyers and sellers will benefit economically, if people who receive goods or services value the money they give up less than they value the good or service they receive in return. Market prices reflect only the specific price levels at which goods or services are of equal marginal or added economic value to both sellers and buyers—the prices at which supply is equal to demand. Buyers and sellers together establish market prices or economic values, which depend on their individual willingness and ability to exchange or trade goods and services.

The creation of additional or new economic value is most commonly associated with the processes of production or manufacturing, which transform less economically valuable natural and human resources into more valuable end products or services. Transformation creates economic value by changing the form or physical characteristics of products or services. Products are transformed by manufacturing or processing, whereas personal services are transformed through experience, education, or training. The benefits from such increases in value typically are shared among consumers, producers, and owners of the basic natural and human resources. Those who have greater ability to influence market prices at various stages of the process typically receive most of the economic benefits associated with changes in form.

The same physical good or personal service may be scarcer in one geographic location than in another and thus of greater economic value. In such cases, transportation or relocation creates new economic value by moving a given product or service from a lower- to a higher-value location. Products are typically shipped from one location to another, whereas people who provide personal services may have to physically relocate to realize new economic opportunities. Again, those who transport or relocate the product or service and those who buy it may share benefits from the increase in value more or less equally in market economies.

A given form of product or service in a given location may be scarcer at one time than at another and thus of different values at different times. For example, the supply of and demand for a good or service may be seasonal or cyclical in nature. In such cases, economic value can be created by storing a product, withholding a service, or otherwise changing the time at which a given product or service is offered for sale. Economic value also places a premium on the present relative to the future, because of the individual, instrumental, and thus deferred nature of economic value. Thus, economic value also can be created by making a good or service available more quickly, sooner rather than later, as explained in chapter 1. The benefits from increases in time value also may be shared more or less equally among market participants.

In summary, markets can be an efficient means of determining economic value. The economic value of every good or service may be different for different forms, places, and times at which it is exchanged and for every pair of individuals who exchange it. The extent to which different individuals benefit from their unique contributions to the value creation process is dependent on relative bargaining power in the exchange process. The task of determining individual economic values from every good or service exchanged in an economy is inherently dynamic and incredibly complex. Markets obviously function differently under different forms of government. Regardless of the form of government, determination of economic value is a basic function of markets.

Markets Ration, Reward, and Allocate Resources

Markets provide an efficient means of rationing available supplies among potential buyers, rewarding producers for their efforts, and providing economic incentives to guide the allocation of natural and human resources to their highest economic uses. The means by which markets carry out these functions begins with the laws of supply and demand, as discussed in chapter 6. Quantities demanded by buyers and quantities supplied or offered for sale move in opposite directions in response to changes in market prices. As prices go *down*, quantities demanded *increase*, but quantities supplied *decline*. As prices go *up*, quantities demanded *decline*, but quantities supplied *increase*. Changes in market prices, up or down, adjust until the quantity demanded always equals the quantity supplied. No surpluses or shortages remain or exist once a competitive market price has been established.

In market economies, markets determine wage rates for labor, interest rates for capital, rental rates for land and other real estate, and salaries for managers and administrators. Demands for these inputs or factors of production are derived directly from consumer-level prices for the things these resources are used to produce. Higher prices for a given product increase the profits of its suppliers, which in turn increases demand and market prices for the natural and human resources used to produce it. Falling product prices reduce profits, weakening demand and reducing prices for the resources or factors used in production.

The supplies of factors of production or resources respond to prices in the same way as the supplies of consumer products. If wage rates fall in a given sector of the economy, workers move to better-paying jobs elsewhere. As producers in a growing industry attempt to expand production and need more capital, they bid up interest rates and capital flows from other uses to finance their expansion. Thus, productive resources—land, labor, capital, and management—are shifted from one use to another as changing prices make them more or less valuable in producing different goods and services. They are shifted from lower- to higher-valued economic uses. This is the process by which scarce resources are allocated among alternative uses in meeting the needs and wants of consumers.

Markets Facilitate Trade Among Nations

Markets can also allow nations, as well as individuals, to benefit from specialization and trade. Benefits from trade result when trade partners are allowed to express their individual comparative advantages. Returning to the concept of substitutes and choices, the opportunity cost of choosing one alternative is the economic value of the alternative or opportunity forgone. The concept of opportunity costs can be used to understand comparative advantage in terms of economic efficiency.

Individuals or nations are more economically efficient in producing things for which their opportunity costs are lower, meaning they have less-valuable economic alternative uses for their resources. The lack of efficiency in producing some things thus becomes a source of economic efficiency or a comparative advantage in producing others. Even those persons and nations that are very inefficient in producing many different things will have comparative advantages in producing those things for which they are "relatively less inefficient." Total economic costs of production will be lower if individuals and nations specialize in producing things for which they have a comparative advantage, meaning they are relatively less *inefficient*, and trading with others to acquire things for which they are relatively more *inefficient* producers.

Markets Provide Incentives for Economic Innovation

Economic value can be created by changing the form, time, place, and possession of goods and services without increasing the quantity of natural or human resources used in the process. Such increases in value do not depend on unsustainable economic growth but do depend on the willingness and ability of entrepreneurs and innovators to take the inevitable risks associated with change or innovation. Risks are an inescapable aspect of change.

Economists distinguish between risks and uncertainties. Risk is the probability or chance of an unfavorable or adverse outcome. To assess risk, decision makers must be able to assess or at least estimate the probability or odds of different possible outcomes so they can identify some specific portion or set of outcomes as being adverse or unfavorable. Uncertainty reflects a lack of knowledge concerning the odds or probabilities of either favorable or unfavorable future outcomes. Under conditions of uncertainty, decision makers must rely on some intuitive or subjective sense of possible outcomes rather than on an objective assessment of different probable outcomes or economic risks.

The potential for profits provides market-based incentives for economic entrepreneurs and innovators to take the risks associated with change. Market-determined costs of productive resources—land, labor, capital, and management—reflect their expected economic values, as determined by competition among producers. If the outcome of an innovation or change turns out better than market expectations, the result will be a profit for the innovator. The resulting increase in economic value will be greater than the economic cost of making the change. If the outcome is worse than market expectations, the result will be a loss. Any economic value created will be less than the economic cost of the change. Cost is determined by market expectations at the time a decision to produce is made; value is determined at the time the product is placed on the market. Again, economic value is deferred value. The difference between the two is either a profit or loss. The potential for profits provides the motivation for entrepreneurs to risk loss.

Markets Create Opportunities for Profits

The term profit is often associated with various measures of benefits relative to costs—most commonly, returns over cash costs, over variable or avoidable costs, or over total costs—which includes sunk or fixed costs. Profit, in the purest sense, is a reward or return for taking the risk of making economic investments or commitments with unknown outcomes, rather than making the same investments in or commitments to essentially risk-free ventures. In a sense, profit is a return over risk-free opportunity costs. An economic loss is the consequence of taking a risk, and failing to realize a profit, rather than accepting a risk-free return.

Economic insolvency is the consequence of taking risks that result in economic losses that exceed the total economic resources or borrowing capacity of the investor. As a result, those with large amounts of capital or borrowing capacity have a natural advantage in making riskier investments that also have greater opportunities for profits. They are less likely to become insolvent even when they suffer large losses, giving them opportunities to more than offset even large losses with future high-risk investments. This is a primary cause of the inevitable concentration of income and wealth among a few large investors in market economies.

Risk and uncertainty are inherent aspects of living, dynamic, evolving systems, including economies and societies. Thus risk taking is an essential aspect of economic sustainability, as are the profits that reward those who are willing and able to take risks. These are "necessary" profits. Such profits are fundamentally different from the "unnecessary" profits stemming from the lack of economic competitiveness that typically exists in market economies. Most market economies today fail to reflect the essential competitive conditions, as will be discussed. Nonetheless, a basic function of markets it to provide incentives for investors to take the inevitable risks associated with economic innovation.

Essential Characteristics of Markets in Sustainable Economies

Markets can be an efficient and effective means of serving the collective interest of individuals within society only to the extent that they are characterized by the specific conditions of economic competition. For markets to function effectively within a sustainable economy, they must conform to the basic conditions of economic competitiveness. First, there must be many buyers and sellers in each market. Second, it must be easy for sellers of new products to enter markets and easy for existing sellers to exit markets. Third, buyers and sellers must have accurate information regarding products and terms of sale. Finally buyers and sellers must be free to act or trade without being subjected to persuasion or coercion.

Economically competitive markets must have so many buyers and sellers that actions of any individual buyer or seller would have no appreciable or significant effect on market prices. This is necessary to ensure that benefits from increases in economic efficiency and reduced costs are passed on to consumers in the form of lower prices rather than retained as excess profits by suppliers. Under competitive conditions, any seller who keeps prices high to enhance profits will lose sales to competitors with lower prices. The basic purpose of economic competition is to minimize prices paid by consumers rather than allow producers to retain excess profits.

Ease of market entry and exit is necessary to ensure that producers with better products, services, or ideas are able to replace those with inferior products, services, or ideas as consumers' needs, tastes, and preferences change. Suppliers must be able to respond effectively and efficiently to inevitable changes in consumer demand. Again, the objective is to ensure that consumers have choices from an assortment or collection of different products and services that include those with the greatest potential economic value at the lowest feasible costs.

To reflect economic value accurately, buyers must be able to anticipate the value they ultimately will receive from a product or service at the time they make their purchase decisions. They must have accurate information regarding not only form, time, and place, but also the ability of a good or service to provide current and continuing benefits to them individually. Lacking such information, their choices will not reflect their true needs, tastes, or preferences and thus will not reflect the true economic value of the good or service.

Finally, buyers must be free to make choices in the absence of intimidation or coercive pressures, such as aggressive marketing tactics or persuasive advertising. Any form of coercion or deception can alter consumers' perceptions of needs or change their tastes and preferences. Expenditures made for advertisements that "create" previously nonexistent consumer demand represent economic wastes, if not outright economic fraud. New markets can be "discovered," rather than "created," without persuasive pressures. Potential buyers need only be informed of the essential characteristics of new products. Sustainable market economies must accept consumers' tastes and preferences as given. To ensure accurate determination of economic value, the consumer must be sovereign.

Market Efficiency: Operational and Allocative

Market economies are characterized by two distinctly different types of efficiency. Operational efficiency reflects the technical efficiency of production and can be measured in terms of output and price. Allocation efficiency reflects the effectiveness with which markets provide consumers with an assortment of goods and services capable of best meeting their individual wants and needs from a limited endowment of natural and human resources.

Economies with lower overall production costs are able to produce larger quantities of economic output at lower prices and thus may be more operationally efficient. Specialization, standardization, and consolidation of control—which characterize industrial production—are means of increasing operational efficiency through "economies of scale." A few large economic organizations may have lower average costs than would a larger number of small operations. Thus, markets with fewer large operations may appear to be more economically efficient, if each operation keeps its profit margins temporarily low while vying for a larger share of the market. However, once a few large operations gain control over a market, they invariably find ways to increase profits, through formal or informal collusion, thus depriving consumers of the economic benefits of their greater operational efficiency.

The effectiveness of markets in meeting the individual needs and wants of society depends on the efficiency of resource allocation—on allocative efficiency—as well as the technical efficiency of production. Ultimately, allocative efficiency depends on maintaining highly competitive markets. There is no means of ensuring the allocative efficiency of markets other than through large numbers of relatively small buyers and sellers, ease of market entry and exit, accurate consumer information, and consumer sovereignty. The efficiency of the allocative process depends on the extent to which actual market conditions conform to the conditions of pure or perfect economic competition. Excessive profits, anywhere in the system, distort price signals and lead to misallocation of productive resources in relation to consumers' needs and preferences.

Today's Markets: Efficient but Not Effective

Today's global economy is dominated by larger corporate organizations that have gained their economic and political power by proclaiming their superiority in *operational* efficiency. They claim their size is necessary to achieve the "economies of scale" necessary to produce goods and services at the lowest possible costs. However, in the process of consolidating production into fewer and larger economic organizations, primarily large public corporations, many of today's markets have lost their *allocative* efficiency. There is no longer any assurance that global markets are allocating scarce natural and human resources efficiently to meet even the *collective* needs of individuals within society.

Admittedly, if the producers and sellers of goods and services are too small, too numerous, or too disorganized to achieve economies of scale, markets may exhibit a lack of operational efficiency. The primary threat to economic sustainability today, however, is that producers and sellers of goods and services are too few, too large, or too organized to ensure effective economic competition. Such markets invariably exhibit a lack of allocative efficiency. An effective balance of allocative and operational efficiency is essential to overall economic efficiency and economic sustainability. However, even the most efficient markets would be capable of meeting only the *collective* needs of individuals and still would not serve the *common* or public interests of society as a whole.

Free Trade Requires Economic Sovereignty

Sustainable "free trade" requires that both parties be "free to not trade"—if they choose not to trade. Nations must be economically sovereign. They must be free to trade only when they believe it is to their benefit to do so. Nations will often find it to their benefit to trade rather than not trade, but they must be selective in choosing when and with whom to trade. They must be free from economic and political pressures or any other form of coercion from other nations. International debts and military agreements, for example, may create trade obligations that interfere with free trade. Both parties to a trade also must have accurate information regarding the ultimate consequences of entering into a trading relationship. Nations must be aware of the ultimate impacts of trade agreements on their natural resources and their people. International trade that is promoted as a means of economic development but instead leads to economic extraction and exploitation is not free trade. In the same way that mutually beneficial trade can take place only between informed, sovereign individuals, international free trade can take place only between informed, sovereign nations.

Sustainable trade among nations must reflect the same fundamental principles that characterize relationships within healthy living systems. As indicated previously, healthy living systems are characterized by selective or semipermeable boundaries. The cells of living organisms are defined by semipermeable cell walls that allow some things in and keep other things out and allow some things out and keep other things in. Living organisms in turn are defined by skins or surfaces that are selective in terms of what is allowed in and out. Without this selectivity, a living organism cannot survive—it is not sustainable. Sustainable communities, economies, and societies likewise must be selective in their relationships with other communities, economies, and societies. The necessary condition for mutually beneficial trade among nations is essentially the same as the necessary conditions for economically competitive markets.

Other Essential Characteristics of Global Markets

Mutually beneficial trade also depends on an absence of unresolved conflicts of interest within trading nations. Unlike individuals, nations are made up of many different people with many different opportunities and internal dependencies. Thus, nations have inherent difficulties in trading relationships because some individuals within nations may benefit from a trade while others may not benefit or may even suffer economically. Even if the nation as a whole benefits economically, economic value does not reflect important social and ethical values, such as the need for social equity and justice. Thus, conflicts of economic interest within nations must be resolved by other means to ensure sustainable benefits from trade.

Mutually beneficial trade also depends on the absence of distortions in relative currency values. Individuals typically use a common currency when they negotiate a trade; however, trade among countries often involves different currencies. Exchange rates among different currencies may be distorted by domestic policy priorities, such as increasing the supply of money to stimulate economic growth or reducing the money supply to control inflation. Thus, currency exchange rates at any given time may distort the underlying comparative advantages among nations, thus distorting the potential gains from trade.

The potential gains from trade based on comparative advantage also depend on the immobility or fixed nature of resources within nations. Items that individuals can offer for trade reflect their unique set of talents, abilities, and productive resources, and thus reflect their comparative advantages. In today's global economy, capital, technology, and even labor may move quite easily among nations, thus distorting the economic concepts of comparative advantage and potential gains from trade. People can immigrate to other countries rather than apply their comparative advantage to the benefit of their native country. Corporate investors can move their capital and technology from nations with higher opportunity costs to nations with lower opportunity costs, rather than investing in economic enterprises in which their nations have comparative advantages. Important differences between today's global economy and the essential economic assumptions of mutually beneficial "free trade" challenge the validity of most assertions regarding the benefits of economic globalization.

Markets that lack economic competitiveness—whether domestic or international—provide opportunities for those in a stronger bargaining position to extract excess profits by exploiting their customers, employees, suppliers, and society in general. Competitive markets must have a large number of buyers and sellers, freedom of entry and exit, accurate information, and economic sovereignty. Economic competitiveness eliminates the possibility of economic advantage based on anything other than being better able to provide economically valuable products or services. In the absence of effective completion, profits are not earned by taking the necessary risks of advancement or betterment, but instead are extorted from society. Thus, sustainable market economies must maintain the conditions of economic competitiveness to ensure that profits reward sustainable economic development rather than exploitative economic growth. Maintaining economic competitiveness is an essential function of government. Sustainable economies must acknowledge and respect the essential function of government as well as the essential characteristics of markets.

Study and Discussion Guide for Individual Readers and Group Leaders or Instructors

- Search the Internet or a library for at least two culturally appropriate textbooks about, or comprehensive references to, market economies. Read the introductory sections or chapters to find the authors' definitions of the basic function of markets. Examine the tables of contents and note which topics covered in this chapter are included in the textbook or Internet reference.

- Identify at least two examples of current public issues arising from a failure to recognize the essential characteristics of markets in sustainable economies. For at least one of these issues, list the specific essential characteristics mentioned in this chapter that markets fail to reflect.

Questions for Individual Reflection or Group Discussion

- Do you believe that all current national economies are mixed economies that include elements of both market and planned economies? If so, what leads you to this conclusion?
- What do you think are the most important functions of markets?
- Is the economic value created by trade among individuals real or an illusion? Explain.
- Explain in your own words how markets determine economic value.
- Explain in your own words the difference between operational and allocative efficiency.
- Do you think "free trade" exists among nations anywhere in today's global economy? If so, where? If not, why not?
- Do you think some profits are necessary? Why or why not?
- Why are your answers to these questions important to the people of your nation, your community, and to you personally?
- After thinking about these questions, what might you do differently to make life better, for others and for yourself?

8

Essential Functions of Government for Economic Sustainability

Ensuring Autonomy and Equity

Government is essential for economic sustainability. The most essential function of government, regardless of the form of government, is to ensure autonomy and equity. The needs of individuals for autonomy or liberty must be balanced with the needs of societies for equity or justice. An efficient economy can serve the collective interests of individuals within society, but an effective government is essential to ensure the common interests of the society as a whole. In addition, while both are necessary, the common good of society must be given priority over the economic good of individuals to accommodate the hierarchy of sustainability.

Social autonomy requires that people be afforded the right to relate freely with other people and with nature, as long as their relationships meet the standards of their society as administered by their government. Within the hierarchy of nature, the integrity of society must take priority over the preferences of individuals. In other words, individual freedoms must be consistent with the greater good of society as a whole. For example, virtually all cultures agree that individual autonomy does not include the freedom to cheat, rob, enslave, or murder.

Social equity requires that standards of behavior, as defined by society, be administered and enforced impartially and fairly to ensure justice for all. People need not be rewarded for exceeding the standards of acceptable social behavior; however, violations of minimum standards must be penalized or prohibited to preserve the integrity of society. A dynamic tension invariably exists between autonomy and equity in all societies, the balance continually shifting with changes in the ecological, social, or economic environment.

Ensuring Economic Autonomy and Equity: Competitive Markets

Economic autonomy and equity can be ensured by economically competitive markets functioning within the constraints of an equitable and just society. Buyers and sellers in such markets have the freedom to act independently, as long as their behavior meets the standards established by their society. Economic equity requires that market participants be rewarded in relation to their ability to contribute economic value to the economy. Economic equity depends on the efficiency of markets, specifically their allocative efficiency, which depends on their competitiveness.

Historically, governments have relied on measures of market structure, conduct, and performance to guide their efforts to maintain competitive markets. Market structure refers to the number and size of economic organizations or business firms participating in a given market. Market conduct refers to the presence or absence of collusion or collaboration among those firms, including price fixing and various market-sharing arrangements. Market performance is measured in terms of market prices and total quantity of production.

The historical economic assumption has been that markets with a large number of small firms would produce larger quantities of products or services at lower prices and, thus, would perform better than markets with fewer larger organizations or firms. Also, markets where firms do not conspire or collude to raise prices would produce greater quantities of output at lower prices than would markets where firms collude in setting prices. Thus, larger numbers of market participants, in the absence of collusion, would result in better market performance.

Over time, market economists have begun to focus more directly on market performance, reasoning that if markets performed well, there was little cause for concern about market structure or conduct. A small number of large economic organizations might have greater operational efficiency, which means they could produce a larger output at a lower price than could a larger number of smaller enterprises. Some economists also add product innovation to their criteria for market performance, since competition also provides incentives for innovation. However, as suggested previously, a small number of large corporations striving for increased market share may *appear* to be superior in terms of market performance, even as they gain greater market power and move further away from the necessary conditions for overall economic efficiency.

As is evident from the history of market economies, the only way governments can ensure both operational and coordinative efficiency is to maintain competitive market *structure*—meaning large numbers of small economic enterprises. If firms are large enough or few enough to have significant individual impacts on market prices or other conditions of trade, history has shown they will find ways to use their market power to retain excess profits by exploiting their customers and/or suppliers. If economies of scale are large enough to make a small number of large economic organizations necessary to serve the public interest, such organizations should be owned and operated by governments or as public utilities under strict government regulation and control. Governments cannot allow operational efficiency to take precedence over allocative efficiency if they are to perform their essential function of maintaining economic equity.

Managing the Money Supply

Management of currency is another essential function of government. The use of money or currency facilitates economic efficiency and thus serves the public interest. In complex societies, it is much more efficient to exchange currency than to exchange the actual goods or services represented by the currency. Without money, those who have something to exchange for something of greater value would have to find someone who had something they valued more who was also willing to trade it to them in return. The economic values of different goods and services can be expressed in terms of currency value, which facilitates economic choices for potential buyers and sellers. Obviously, buying and selling is generally far easier and more efficient than is bartering for many goods and services among large numbers of individuals.

Money also can be used as a store of economic value, in that money received in exchange for goods or services need not be exchanged immediately for other goods or services. Money saved, in a sense, is stored economic value. Currencies generally are not perishable and can be saved or stored for indefinite periods. Money also provides a convenient source of credit. Currency that one person saves can be lent to another, with the promise that the loan will be repaid in the future. In a sense, the lender is allowing the borrower to use the economic value he or she has earned but has chosen to store or save for a time. In fact, all currencies issued by governments—paper bills and coins—are loans made to the issuing government. They represent promises made by the government to provide the holder with a stated fixed quantity of economic value in exchange for the paper bill or metal coin. A person who has currency on hand, in a sense, has lent the value of the currency to the government until that person decides to spend it. Spending currency is equivalent to passing the loan made to the government on to someone else.

Because of the time preference of economic value, borrowers generally are willing to pay lenders interest for the privilege of being able to buy something now rather than waiting until later. For the same reason, lenders who defer using their money generally require an interest payment to offset the time-related difference in value. Interest rates, expressed as a percentage of loan values, are market prices of loans that respond to the quantity of money lenders make available relative to the quantity of money borrowers desire. Money facilitates the process of determining market interest rates as well as paying and receiving interest payments on borrowed money.

Stabilizing Prices: Inflation, Deflation

Governments must ensure that adequate quantities of currency are available at all times to facilitate efficient market transactions. If too little currency is available, prices of goods and services will fall in relation to their economic value until they reestablish a stable relationship between the smaller quantity of money and the quantity of goods and services exchanged. This is known as price deflation, meaning it takes less money to buy goods and services of the same economic value as before. Falling prices create an illusion of declining economic value, which can trigger negative expectations and lead to an economic recession. If more money is placed in circulation than is needed for exchange of the goods and services available, prices will rise, reflecting the larger quantity of money in relation to the quantity of goods and services exchanged. This is known as price inflation, meaning it takes more money to buy a given amount of goods and services even though they have not risen in economic value. This creates an illusion of increasing economic value by creating positive expectations that can trigger economic growth but can also lead to economic instability.

If borrowers and lenders are to be able to make efficient economic decisions, they must be able to anticipate any difference in the economic value represented by the currency value of loans at the time loans are made and the currency value at the time they are to be repaid. Lacking this information, neither borrowers nor lenders are able to make logical economic decisions. Currency values need not be constant, but they do need to be predictable. If lenders and borrowers can count on a given, stable rate of price inflation or deflation, changes in currency values can be reflected in higher or lower interest rates. Unpredictable currency values can destroy borrowers' and lenders' confidence in the economy and lead to economic chaos or collapse.

Creating Money

Money is created any time money that has been saved, or otherwise taken "out of circulation," spent, or lent to someone else. Individuals, businesses, governments, and other economic entities typically deposit their money in banks or other similar financial institutions. Depositors may consider their money to be in savings. However, banks can create money by putting money on deposit back into circulation by lending it to borrowers. The depositors still have money in the bank and the borrowers have new money to spend. Bank deposits serve the same purpose as any other form of currency or money. Thus, banks create new money by putting bank deposits into circulation. Central governments also can increase the total amount of money in circulation by depositing money in commercial banks or other lending institutions. The banks are then able to create additional money by putting the government deposits into circulation through new loans to borrowers.

Governments typically establish what is known as fractional reserve requirements to ensure that banks keep enough in reserve to accommodate those who might want to withdraw their deposits on any given day. A reserve requirement of 10 percent means a bank can only lend out a maximum of 90 percent of the amount of money it has on deposit. The portion of an initial deposit a bank typically lends is spent by the borrowers and eventually ends up in someone else's deposit accounts in either the same or another bank. The banks can then lend a portion of the new deposits where the lent money was deposited. This process can continue indefinitely. Each new loan linked with a given initial deposit will be smaller than the last if there is a reserve requirement. This process continues as long as the initial deposit remains in the initial bank, typically multiplying the amount of money in circulation in relation to the amount of the initial deposit. With a reserve requirement of 10 percent, the maximum amount of new money would be approximately ten times as large as the initial deposit.

Whenever deposits are withdrawn from banks and "taken out of circulation," the whole process must be reversed. Each loan must be recalled and repaid to repay the full amount of the initial deposit. Banks count on the fact that large numbers of depositors generally do not withdraw money from circulation in large amounts at any given time. Thus, banks are typically able to pay deposits on demand and reduce their loans in an orderly fashion when deposits are withdrawn. If irresponsible lending results in many borrowers not being able to repay their loans, the financial system becomes vulnerable to collapse. Governments may insure commercial bank deposits as a means of assuring depositors that their money is safe in banks to avoid sudden or disorderly withdrawals. So-called runs on the banks can destroy confidence in a nation's currency.

As indicated previously, individuals typically spend the money they withdraw from banks, or they take money out of banks and deposit or invest it with other lending institutions. Such withdrawals don't actually take money out of circulation; it is still available for loans. Governments, however, can easily take money out of circulation and occasionally do so to reduce an economy's total money supply. Governments can withdraw deposits from banks and reduce the number of deposits available to support loans, much as governments deposit money in banks to make more money available for loans. Anything that increases or decreases the total amount of loans increases or decreases the amount of currency or money in circulation.

Regulating Financial Institutions

Anyone who makes a loan increases the quantity of money in circulation, which increases the total money supply. Individuals typically do not lend enough money to create a problem for governments in regulating the total money supply. However, large, unregulated private lending institutions can have dramatic effects on the total money supply of a nation and even global financial markets, as they did in the early 2000s. When private investment banking or lending institutions "buy loans" from a government-regulated bank, they are essentially lending the money previously lent by the bank, freeing the bank to make other loans, thus increasing the money supply. In addition, investments in financial institutions can be used to create money just as effectively as deposits in banks, without the same public scrutiny or regulation.

Instability of currency values is probably a greater threat to the sustainability of national economies than any other single type of economic mismanagement. The existence of currency, while necessary to facilitate market transactions, requires effective government oversight and regulation to prevent deception, exploitation, and outright fraud. Incompetent government officials can create financial chaos by placing too much or too little currency in circulation. Borrowers may be encouraged to borrow more money than they can repay by those who will benefit from the loans but will not bear the consequences of the borrowers' default. Lenders may be encouraged by high interest rates to lend money to finance ventures that have no chance of success. Large financial institutions can make large profits by creating money without the public responsibility of a regulated banking system. Thus, governments must carefully regulate all lending institutions. Governments, not private investment firms, must have sole authority and responsibility for maintaining the integrity of currencies. Economic efficiency depends on the integrity of currency, which is an essential economic responsibility of government.

Coordinating Monetary and Fiscal Policies

Government policies related to stabilizing currency values are typically referred to as "monetary policies." Government policies related to taxing and spending are called "fiscal policy." The economic costs of government must be paid by the members of society, through various forms of taxation. Governments have the power to save money or borrow money. So a government can either run a budget deficit, meaning that it spends more than it taxes, or run a surplus, meaning it taxes more than it spends. Governments can also balance their budgets. Deficit spending can stimulate private economic activity through government jobs and contracts that create private investment opportunities. Budget surpluses have the opposite effect on national economies. Thus, effective fiscal policies can be quite useful, sometimes essential, in stabilizing overall economic activity. However, governments have a natural tendency to run deficits rather than surpluses. The short-run economic benefits of expansion are greater than the long-run economic benefits of economic stability. Persistent budget deficits often result in large "national debts" that create economic obligations for future generations their governments may not be able to meet.

Requiring governments to maintain balanced budgets might be considered a logical means of ensuring intergeneration fiscal equity. However, in times of deep economic recession, governments have no means of stimulating economic recovery other than deficit spending. A balanced budget requirement would eliminate fiscal policy as a means of stabilizing national economies. Monetary and fiscal policy must work together to ensure the effectiveness of either. It is counterproductive to maintain high interest rates and large government deficits at the same time. Likewise, it is counterproductive to run large surpluses while a government is increasing its money supply to stimulate economic recovery. Economic stability is a legitimate and necessary function of government to ensure economic efficiency. Monetary and fiscal policy must function in harmony to facilitate economic sustainability.

Internalizing Economic "Externalities"

Governments must also cope with instances of "market failure." Some economic costs and benefits associated with decisions accrue to someone other than the economic decision maker. Such costs and benefits typically are called economic "externalities," meaning they occur outside or "external" to the markets where they originate. All externalities are either ecological or social because nature and society are the only sources of economic value. Employment is probably the most common external economic benefit, in that society, as well as employers, benefits from employment. Environmental pollution is a common example of external costs. Pollution may reduce the economic value of property and the productive capacity of people subjected to its negative effects. External costs result in markets overvaluing the net economic benefits associated with market-based decisions. External benefits result in markets undervaluing the net economic benefits of market-based decisions. An essential function of government is to "internalize economic externalities," particularly external costs, to ensure that decision makers consider the full economic consequences of their decisions.

Governments may use a variety of means to ensure that markets accurately reflect economic values. The most straightforward approach to internalizing external costs is to enact government prohibitions. Such prohibitions prevent any individual or economic organization from carrying out activities that impose social or environmental costs on other individuals or on society as a whole. Other approaches include penalties, fines, and taxes to compensate individuals or societies that suffer the consequences of economic externalities. Regardless of the government policies or strategies used, the basic purpose is to require investors to consider the full economic costs of their choices.

Ensuring Employment Opportunities

A market economy will not ensure adequate employment opportunities to allow all people who are willing and able to work to meet their basic economic needs. Economic value is determined at the consumer level. As a result, economic resources in market economies are allocated or directed to meet the needs of people as consumers rather than as workers. The basic needs and preferences of the consumers within a society do not necessarily coincide or match the basic needs and preferences of the workers within the same society. For example, those with greater incomes or wealth have a disproportionate influence on the products produced by a society and, consequently, the nature of employment opportunities. Such income and wealth often results from greater access to capital, rather than greater productive capacity as a laborer, manager, or entrepreneur. In the absence of government involvement, some workers in a market economy inevitably are forced to accept employment that is economically exploitive or socially degrading to produce things of adequate economic value to meet their basic needs. Others are left without employment, either periodically or permanently. Ensuring opportunities for all people to meet their basic needs through employment that is neither degrading nor exploitive is an essential function of government.

Corporations and other economic organizations routinely try to coerce governments to compensate them for providing employment opportunities. They claim that providing employment is an external benefit for which they are not adequately compensated, and they lobby governments for employment-related subsidies and/or tax credits. However, it would be equally as logical for workers to demand government subsidies or tax credits to compensate them for providing their services to their employers. Employers are no more or less important to the economy overall than are their workers. When individuals and organizations create external economic benefits, they obviously are adequately compensated for doing so.

If additional employment in necessary for the common good of society, it is more logical for government to provide additional public employment than to subsidize or incentivize additional private employment. Times of high unemployment provide ideal opportunities to employ more government workers to replace public infrastructure, such as transportation and information systems, and to make the long-term social and ecological investments necessary for economic sustainability, as in education and renewable energy. In the hierarchy of sustainability, the common good of society must take priority over economic incentives for individuals. Furthermore, economies do not generate sufficient surplus to reward everyone economically for everything they must do for the common good of society and humanity.

Regulating International Trade

Negotiation and regulation of international trade is another essential economic function of government. Governments have the same basic responsibility for maintaining the conditions of economic competition in international trade as they do in domestic markets. To benefit from a global economy, nations must maintain their economic sovereignty. They must maintain alternative sources for the things they choose to buy and alternative markets for the things they choose to sell. They must be willing and able to enter new markets and exit from current markets as their comparative advantages change over time. They must have access to adequate information to assess the ultimate impacts of their international trade and investment decisions on people and on natural resources. They must be able to trade only when it is to their benefit to do so.

The hierarchy of sustainability is also relevant to trade among nations in the global economy. Governments must demand the right and accept the responsibility of protecting their people and their natural resources from exploitation by outside economic interests. Nations benefit from trade only when trade results in mutual benefits to the people of both trading nations. Trade can increase the economic efficiency with which global resources are allocated among alternative uses, but *economic* autonomy and efficiency cannot be allowed to take precedence over *social* autonomy and equity. The sustainability of a given nation's natural and human resources is essential to its economic sustainability. Conservation and protection of a nation's common sources of wealth is an essential function of that nation's government in negotiating and regulating international trade.

Maintaining Market Infrastructure

To facilitate economic equity, governments also must accept responsibility for developing and maintaining the legal infrastructure necessary for markets to function effectively and efficiently. Market transactions depend on the existence of legal rights to own and exchange private property and on legally enforceable commitments or contracts between buyers and sellers and between borrowers and lenders. Economic competition also depends on the availability of accurate market information and rules and regulations to deal with potential deception, fraud, or intimidation. In cases where exchanges can be negotiated electronically, networks for transferring information and money must be secure from all types of malicious manipulation. Information regarding prices and conditions of exchange in various alternative markets must be publicly available to all potential buyers and sellers to ensure competition. All of these are legitimate and essential economic functions of government.

Ensuring Social Autonomy and Equity

Some *noneconomic* functions of governments are essential for economic sustainability because social equity is fundamentally different from economic equity and both are essential for economic sustainability. Governments serve

the same basic functions for communities and societies that cultures serve for families and friendships. Cultural values evolve over time to shape individual behaviors in ways that have proven necessary to serve the common good of families, friendships, and communities. Different cultures are defined by standards of normal and acceptable behavior that have been passed down from generation to generation within different social or cultural groups.

Cultures also evolve to reflect behaviors that people have found necessary to survive and thrive in particular geographic locations or regions. Thus, cultures define acceptable ecological human relationships with nature as well as social relationships among humans. Cultures that condemn ecological exploitation, for example, reflect life experiences within societies that have persisted in particular places over extended periods. Within families, friendships, and small cohesive communities, cultural standards of behavior are defined and enforced through various social pressures and sanctions. Within larger and less cohesive communities and societies, cultural standards must be defined and enforced through government.

In general, the greater part of the total value of human relationships is not economic value but instead is purely social and ethical value. Great philosophers throughout human history have generally agreed: the most important benefits of human relationships arise from fulfillment of the basic needs of humans to be accepted, respected, and esteemed by people whom they in turn accept, respect, and esteem. People also must be free to relate to other people in socially responsible ways if they are to meet this basic human need. Social autonomy and equity are essential prerequisites for sustaining the integrity of societies within which sustainable economies must function.

Restraining Economic Exploitation

Legal regulations or restraints are absolutely necessary to restrain economic exploitation of nature and society. That said, a societal consensus must support such regulations and restraints. Such restraints can only ensure that the many people who would voluntarily conform to the cultural standards of their society don't have to compete with the few who would not. Neither families nor communities nor governments can ensure that a society will realize the full potential benefits of positive social relationships. However, the absence of social autonomy and equity precludes any possibility of the social benefits essential for sustainability. The possibility of social and ethical rewards and the certainty of societal or government penalties motivate individuals to make the *noneconomic* decisions necessary to sustain the productivity of nature and society. Real people may or may not respond willingly to such motivations. Organizations that are purely economic, such as large, publicly traded corporations, have no social or ethical values; they are not human. Governments must protect those who would choose ecologically and socially responsible behavior from those who will not or cannot.

In other words, governments cannot ensure economic sustainability, but they can provide the social and ecological environment within which autonomous individuals can choose to work individually and together to ensure sustainability. Governments cannot endow people with the courage to be trustworthy and kind in their relationships with other people, but governments can ensure social autonomy and the institutional means necessary for people to ensure social equity and justice for all. Governments cannot endow people with an ecological conscience, but governments can allow people to reflect the ecological principles of holism, diversity, and interdependence in establishing laws and administering regulations. The economy must not be allowed to degrade the integrity or deplete the productivity of either society or nature. Only people working together through government can perform this essential function for economic sustainability.

Maintaining the Consent of the Governed

The essential social functions of governments typically are defined in terms of rights and responsibilities, which generally are encoded or expressed in national charters or constitutions. Such documents define the requirements of citizenship, including what is required from citizens in support of their nation and what citizens can expect from their nation in return. These documents may be developed by individuals, small groups of national leaders, or through public processes involving broad-based input from the citizenry. However, such documents are effective only to the extent that they reflect a "consensus of the governed."

A monarch or dictator can govern a nation only so long as the people governed consent to accept their rights and responsibilities as defined and administered by their ruler. Lacking such consent, the people eventually will demand a fundamental change in government. The demanded change may come quickly or slowly, but it inevitably will come. The process of change may or may not be peaceful. If restoring a consensus requires an armed rebellion, the process will take longer and will be more difficult, painful, and costly to the nation, but it eventually will come. Regardless, no government can sustain its power to govern without the consent of the governed.

A consensus does not require unanimity or complete agreement. It does require agreement among a sufficiently large majority, however, to convince the rest of the people that it is in their best interest to support, rather than oppose, the majority. There will always be a few people in any society who refuse to consent, but their numbers must be small enough not to interfere with the effective functioning of government. A consensus in support of certain basic rights and responsibilities of the governed is essential for economic sustainability. These rights and responsibilities may be expressed in a wide variety of ways, but they must reflect the essential *principles* of economic sustainability.

Various nations have chosen various ways of expressing the rights and responsibilities of citizenship. The United Nations (UN) General Assembly has adopted and proclaimed "The Universal Declaration of Human Rights," in an attempt to reach an international consensus in support of a set of thirty Articles expressing the rights and responsibilities of "global citizenship." Most nations of the world have embraced, at least in concept, many of the rights in the thirty different Articles, but no nation has fully embraced them all. Some nations vigorously advocate and protest violations of some specific human rights in the UN proclamation while openly denying and violating other rights on the UN list. The freedom of all to express their personal opinions and the right of all to the economic necessities of life are particularly contentious issues among nations. There is no global consensus yet regarding the basic social, economic, or ecological rights of people to be ensured through processes of government. Ensuring basic human rights remains, and perhaps will remain, the responsibility of individual nations and cultures.

Balancing Rights and Responsibilities

With every right comes an equal responsibility. The citizens of societies that grant equal rights to future generations must be willing to bear the economic costs of restraining their current economic extractions from nature and exploitation of society. Citizens of societies that grant to all the right to the economic necessities of life must be willing to tax those who have more than enough, including themselves, to ensure that others have enough to meet their basic needs. Economic equity would require taxing each individual in proportion to his or her income or wealth. Social equity requires taxing individuals to reflect the specific social and ethical values of the particular society, rather than the socially indifferent values of economic equity.

As suggested previously, individuals have inherently unequal abilities and opportunities to earn and accumulate economic wealth. The possession of unequal wealth creates a natural economic advantage to acquiring even more wealth. Wealthy people have the capacity to absorb the risk of periodic losses associated with investments that have the potential for accumulating ever greater wealth. This natural tendency toward concentration of wealth eventually leads to the concentration of both economic and political power that threatens both economic and social equity. Thus, the intentional and purposeful redistributions of income and wealth, through progressive taxes on incomes and estates in market economies, are essential responsibilities of governments for economic sustainability. Socially equitable distribution of income and wealth has proven to be one of the most difficult functions of governments with both market and planned economics.

Those who lack the ability to contribute their share to societal good economically must be required to contribute in other ways. All people who are physically and mentally able to contribute to their own well-being have a responsibility to do so to the extent they are able. In so doing, they are minimizing the economic burden placed on the rest of society. Every physically able person is capable of performing some type of useful public service and might logically be required to do so as a means of fulfilling his or her public responsibility. Such contributions might be a logical alternative to paying taxes for those who are not capable of contributing their full share economically—to the extent their contributions exceed the public services required from everyone else. Different societies may have very different social values. However, every right society grants to individuals carries with it a responsibility of individuals to society that must be fulfilled by one means or another, regardless of the society.

Ensuring Rights of Future Generations

The rights most essential for economic sustainability are the rights of future generations. Meeting the economic needs of the present without diminishing economic opportunities for the future ultimately depends on those of current and future generations being afforded equal rights. Government's public *responsibilities* to maintain the efficiency, resilience, and regenerative capacities of natural and human resources are derived directly from the *rights* of future generations. An essential function of governments for economic sustainability is ensuring equal rights for both current and future generations.

The simplest and most direct means of ensuring the rights of future generations would be through an article in national charters or constitutions stating that those of current and future generations are to be afforded equal rights and opportunities. Each law or regulation would then have to be examined, not only with respect to protecting the rights of those of current generations, but also with respect to their potential impacts on the rights of future generations. For example, regulations regarding greenhouse gas emissions and depletion of fossil energy would have to be evaluated in terms of their potential impacts on the economic opportunities of future generations.

Discretionary Functions of Government

Governments can perform many useful functions in addition to those essential for autonomy and equity. Anything that furthers or promotes the public or common good, but for which individual or economic incentives are either absent or inadequate, represents a legitimate "public good or service." Economists generally limit public goods and services to those things of impersonal, instrumental value to individuals that are "not scarce" and thus have no economic value. In contemporary economics, all public goods and services are defined as having two closely related characteristics: *nonrival* and *nonexcludable*. Some goods and services have both characteristics, while others have only one or the other.

Nonrival means that people can consume or use as much as they want of something without diminishing the amount available for anyone else. Examples include clean air and a national defense system. Once such goods or services are made available, they are no longer scarce because one person using them doesn't diminish the amount available for others. Nonexcludable means that once something is made available, there is no reasonable means of excluding anyone from its benefits. City streets are an example, as it would be impractical to collect tolls at every street intersection. National defense is both nonrival and nonexcludable. Markets are incapable of allocating natural and human resources to provide such goods or services, because they are not scarce, so they have no market value.

The function of the government in such cases is to allocate the provision and use of such goods and services to maximize economic benefits to society in relation to economic costs paid by society. Economists assume societal well-being can be maximized by maximizing the sum of net economic benefits to individuals, even if some of these benefits have no market value. Government provision of public goods and services is simply viewed as an imperfect substitute for markets in cases where markets fail. There is no recognition of the common social and ethical values of relationships that arise among people within socially equitable and just societies. Economics doesn't address issues of social autonomy and equity.

Anything that contributes to the public good of society represents a legitimate function of government if economic incentives are absent or inadequate. Public roads and transportation systems are common examples of public services. They contribute to the public good even though individual economic incentives are often inadequate to justify their construction. Police protection is another legitimate public service. Once a culture of law and order has been established for a community, everyone benefits, regardless of whether they pay for the police protection. Public education clearly benefits society in addition to the economic benefits it provides for individuals. Some public goods and some levels of public service are necessary to ensure autonomy and equity, but others are purely discretionary. Economic development or growth, for example, is not an essential public service; it is purely discretionary. It is simply more efficient to provide many public goods and services collectively, through government, rather than devising some means of giving them economic value.

Essential Functions Must Take Priority

The distinction between essential and discretionary functions of government is critical to economic sustainability. The economy must generate enough economic value to meet the economic needs of individuals, society, and humanity. The capacities of sustainable economies will always be limited by the sustainable use of their natural and human resources. The capacities of governments will always be limited by the capacities of their economies. In other words, governments will always have limited funds with which to carry out both the essential and discretionary functions of government. The essential functions of government must take priority over the discretionary functions of government if the economy is to function sustainably.

Different cultures will choose different words and expressions to reflect their commitment to working together through government to ensure economic sustainability. However, the principles of economic sustainability are not arbitrary; they are expressions of how nature functions, including how human societies function and how individuals function within societies. The hierarchy of sustainability is the hierarchy of nature. The ethical values of cultures and the social values of societies must take precedence over the economic preferences and priorities of individuals. Governments must balance the needs for economic and social autonomy and equity with the capacities of nature and humanity to create a social context within which economies can function sustainably.

Study and Discussion Guide for Individual Readers and Group Leaders or Instructors

- Search the Internet or a library for your national constitution, charter, or other documents associated with the establishment of your government. Examine the documents for references to specific rights and responsibilities of citizenship and for specific references to the economic responsibilities of your government.
- List at least six functions currently performed by your government and assess whether they are essential or discretionary functions of government.
- Search the Internet or a library for at least two references to current public issues having to do with conflicts between government policies related to the economy and government policies related to citizens' rights and responsibilities. For at least one of these issues, list all of the essential functions involved in the conflict or controversy.

Questions for Individual Reflection or Group Discussion

- Do you believe autonomy or equity adequately defines the essential functions of government? Why or why not?
- Explain in your own words how maintaining competitive markets and regulating currency relate to economic autonomy and equity.
- Explain in your own words how money is created and destroyed.
- Do you believe loans by banks and individuals should be allowed to function as currency? If so, why? If not, why not?
- Do you believe social autonomy and equity should take priority over economic autonomy and equity? Why or why not?
- Why is the "consent of the governed" essential for economic sustainability?
- Do you believe in the concept of "universal human rights"? Why or why not?
- Explain in your own words how *discretionary* functions of government are different from *essential* government functions.
- Why are your answers to these questions important to the people of your nation, your community, and to you personally?
- After thinking about these questions, what might you do differently to make life better, for others and for yourself?

The Essential Mission
of Sustainable Economies

Economic Growth Is Not Sustainable

A sustainable economy must arise from and be supported by a consensus of society regarding the essential mission of its economy. Lacking a societal consensus for sustainability, governments cannot sustain the power necessary to protect their natural and human resources from extraction and exploitation. The first step toward a consensus in support of economic sustainability is the realization that an economy that is motivated and driven by the mission of economic growth is not sustainable. The rates of economic growth experienced during the industrial era were an aberration in human history that is unlikely to recur in the future. Global economic growth rates of 2 percent to 3 percent would be considered very modest by industrial era standards. However, with an annual growth rate of only 2.5 percent, the global economy would double in size every thirty years. A global economy with a total economic output equal to only one U.S. dollar two thousand years ago, that had grown at a rate of 2.5 percent per year, would generate an economic output of $3.6 sextillion U.S. dollars today—that is $3.6 followed by twenty zeros. Such an economy would be equivalent to seven billion people spending nearly *one million* dollars every minute of every day. Furthermore, this amount would double over the next thirty years. Obviously, the economic growth rates of the industrial era were an aberration, and such growth rates will not be sustainable in the future.

The economic growth of the industrial era was made possible by an abundance of cheap energy—first, old-growth forests, then surface mining of coal, and for the past hundred years, relatively shallow reservoirs of oil and natural gas. However, most of the world's old-growth forests have been harvested, and much of its remaining coal is deep below the earth's surface or buried within large mountain ranges. Much of its remaining oil and natural gas reserves are deep beneath the floors of oceans or in remote corners of the world hardly touched by civilization. These remaining deposits of fossil energy will require increasing amounts of energy to extract and refine, and the quantities extracted will by necessity be smaller in each future decade. The world is not out of fossil energy, as most estimates indicate that more than half of all the earth's fossil energy deposits remain in the earth. However, the world is quickly running out of the abundant and cheap fossil energy necessary to sustain continuing economic growth.

The global economy today is growing from a much larger economic base than was the case at the onset of the industrial revolution. This means the second half of the earth's fossil energy stocks would be depleted much more quickly than the first, even at the same annual rate of growth as during the industrial era. In addition, the remaining sources of fossil energy are major contributors to greenhouse gasses and other pollutants, which are threatening the ability of the earth's natural ecosystems to support human life. Coal is the largest remaining source of fossil energy and is also the greatest threat to the natural environment. Even the remaining reserves of oil and natural gas pose far larger ecological risks today than they have in the past. Global stocks of "recoverable" and "useful" fossil energy almost certainly will be depleted by the end of this century. Fossil energy reserves could be largely depleted as soon as midcentury, if nations attempt to maintain even current rates of economic growth over the next few decades.

The era of abundant fossil energy is over. The global economy of the next century must be sustained by the daily inflow of new solar energy, rather than the fossil solar energy that was captured and stored in the earth over millions of years. The flow of solar energy available for economic use is relatively constant, but it is finite as well. The sun must support the entire natural ecosystem of the earth, not just the human species. Humans are inherently dependent on energy from other biological sources. Continuing *growth* in the global economy cannot be sustained indefinitely, regardless of how small the rate of economic growth. The energy available from all sustainable sources combined—wind, water, solar panels, biofuels—will be less plentiful and far more costly than fossil energy has been in the past. The global economy may grow during some times in the future and shrink in others. Economies of some nations may expand while others contract. However, economies in general simply cannot sustain economic growth indefinitely. The lack of sustainability in today's global economy is a direct consequence of a global economy striving to create infinite economic wealth in a finite world. Economic growth simply cannot remain the mission of the global economy.

The New Steady State Economy

Some economists have advocated a "steady state economy" as the new economy of the future. A steady state economy must function at a constant or steady rate of resource use or throughput, meaning a constant flow of energy and materials used to produce goods and services. The sustainable level of energy throughput is defined by the ability to sequester useful energy from the total energy inflow and the capacity of nature to absorb, detoxify, or neutralize the outflow of wasted energy. A steady state economy is typically defined as an economy that maintains a constant population, meaning a constant supply of labor and constant stocks of natural and financial capital, including personal wealth. In a steady state economy, there is no growth in total economic output or aggregate personal wealth.

Therefore, the sustainable level of economic wealth on Earth is ultimately limited by the quantity of economic value that can be extracted from the daily inflow of solar energy. All of the molecules of matter on Earth can be recycled or reused over and over again to produce things of economic value. Solar energy can be used to offset the unavoidable loss of usefulness each time the physical elements bound together by energy are released to make the energy available for use. However, all of the energy on Earth at any given time ultimately will be lost through the release of heat back into the rest of the universe—through the process of entropy. All of this lost energy must be replenished with solar energy to maintain economic sustainability.

Over time, the economic usefulness of a given amount of energy can be increased by increasing the efficiency of energy use or the amount of useful energy sequestered from the total energy inflow. This is commonly referred to as "de-linking" production from resource and energy use. However, there are theoretical limits to energy use efficiency. New energy cannot be created and some energy inevitably will be lost to entropy, no matter how efficiently energy is used. Consequently, there are finite limits to the level of economic output that can be sustained on Earth over time. A concept of a steady state economy provides a logical conceptual foundation for the development of a sustainable economy.

A New Mission: Happiness, Quality of Life

Economic sustainability obviously will require a fundamental change in the current mission of increasing income and wealth through continuing economic growth. The logical mission of economic sustainability is the pursuit of human happiness and overall quality of life. Such a change in mission will not likely take place until people—individually, nationally, and globally—have a clear understanding that economic sustainability is a prerequisite to achieving greater happiness and a fundamentally better way of life. Lacking this new vision of a better future—beyond sustainability—most people will continue to support the mission of economic growth.

This change in mission will not come easily but it is certainly both logical and possible. Throughout human history people have known that beyond some basic level of physical and mental well-being, there is no relationship between further increases in income or wealth and increases in happiness or overall quality of life. Once the basic human needs for food, clothing, shelter, health care, and other essentials of life have been met, quality of life depends far more on the quality of social relationships than on the quantity of income or wealth.

Humans are social beings; they need to be accepted, respected, cared for, and loved. Humans are also moral beings; they need a sense of purpose and meaning in life. People need to believe what they are doing is significant, that their actions in some sense are "right and good." Once essential human needs are met, human happiness or quality of life depends far more on cultivating the social and spiritual dimensions of life than on acquiring more income or wealth. The essential mission of a sustainable economy must be to advance individual happiness and overall societal well-being.

Enough to Meet the Needs of All

This new vision for the future must begin with the realization that most people in the world, particularly those in the so-called developed nations, don't need more economic growth. Their economies are already producing far more than enough economic output to meet the basic human needs of their societies. At the time of the industrial revolution, most people in the world were unable to meet their basic human needs, so economic growth at that time was a logical mission for economies. However, that mission has been accomplished, at least for those in the industrial nations of the world. In fact, there has been no indication of further increases in happiness, well-being, or overall satisfaction with life in the so-called developed economies over the past fifty years, in spite of continued growth in income and wealth. For these nations, the "economic problem" has been solved. Some people in these nations are still unable to meet their basic human needs, but only because their society is not fulfilling its responsibility to ensure social equity and justice for all. The logical mission for these economies is to return to the historic mission of humanity, to the pursuit of happiness and quality of life.

Many so-called developing nations of the world still need to focus on their "economic problem," on producing enough to meet the basic human needs of all within their societies. However, these nations need not consume all of the earth's remaining natural resources in the process of developing their economies. In addition, they can develop their economies without sacrificing their cultures, communities, and families. Such nations can balance their necessary economic growth with equally necessary social responsibility and ecological integrity. Sustainable development may be slower and more difficult than industrial development, but in a world running out of fossil energy, sustainable development is the most logical alternative for the future of all nations.

The world obviously cannot sustain continuing human population growth without continuing economic growth. However, the global population need not continue to grow. Growth in human population is inevitably linked in one way or another to a lack of social security. Humans, like other species, have a natural tendency to reproduce, but they only choose to overreproduce when they must rely on their children for trusting and caring relationships or they need to rely on one or more of their children to take care of their needs in their old age. In some cultures, women also lack the security to make their own decisions regarding how many children they will bear and raise. These insecurities are less prevalent in economically developed countries but are not dependent on economic affluence or surplus. All of these insecurities can be addressed through more trusting and caring relationships among people within communities and societies—without economic affluence or wealth. Economic growth and widespread wealth are not necessary to stabilize global population growth.

Many nations have been able to meet the basic human needs of their people with no more than US$10,000 to $15,000 per person of economic output per year. As developing economies have grown beyond this modest level, there has been no consistent relationship between further economic growth and greater happiness or overall well-being. If the global population were stabilized by reduced social insecurities, the earth quite likely would have more than enough resources, including the daily inflow of solar energy, to meet the basic needs of people in both developed and developing countries. The world of the future will have enough energy to sustain a desirable quality of life for humanity, just not have enough energy to sustain the economic growth of the industrial era.

Prosperity Without Growth

A logical expression of the mission for sustainable economies might be "sustainable prosperity." The word "prosperity" is derived from the Latin word for "doing well." Prosperity, or doing well, has social and psychological dimensions as well as an economic dimension. Prosperity depends on positive relationships, respecting and being respected, loving and being loved, contributing useful work and being equitably rewarded, and having a sense of belonging and trust within the larger community and society. Prosperity is closely related to the concepts of happiness, quality of life, or overall well-being. A sustainable economy will be required to sustain prosperity; however, prosperity does not require continual economic growth. The tax revenues needed to support essential government functions need not grow any faster than incomes; aggregate incomes need not grow any faster than growth in populations; and, over time, populations need not grow at all.

The mistaken belief that prosperity requires economic growth is rooted in the fact that human happiness or well-being seems to depend on having some sense of progress or achievement in life. Progress or achievement measured in terms of stronger personal relationships or a greater sense of purpose and meaning is not limited by lack of economic growth. The social and ethical dimensions of happiness require no more than having enough biological energy to fuel the human body and mind. Happiness depends far more on how human energy is used than on how much energy is available. In fact, government policies that promote economic growth are far more likely to compromise rather than enhance the ability of individuals to grow socially and spiritually. Furthermore, if there is an absolute limit to the extent to which human relationships and human ethics can be improved, the limits are so far removed from the current human condition as to be of no practical consequence.

In addition, opportunities would always be available for individual economic progress and achievement within sustainable economies. Beyond some very modest level, the sense of economic success becomes relative rather than absolute. The amount of money people earn or have relative to other people matters far more than their absolute levels of income or wealth. There will always be opportunities for individuals to acquire more wealth, even if the economy overall does not generate more wealth. Economies are inherently dynamic; individuals are constantly making and losing fortunes even during times of economic stagnation or recession. The lack of economic growth does little if anything to diminish the opportunities for individual economic success.

Quality Employment Opportunities

Cyclical unemployment, a natural result of economic dynamics, is often cited as a justification for the mission of economic growth. Growing economies minimize unemployment during cyclical downturns and create full employment for growing populations during periods of economic prosperity. However, the need to increase employment to accommodate economic recessions does not present an insurmountable obstacle to economic sustainability. During inevitable economic downturns, one logical strategy would be to create opportunities for each worker to work fewer hours—to share the available work. This would leave more time for building relationships and contemplation of life's deeper ethical and moral values during economic recessions. Economic recessions could be times of greater personal and spiritual growth.

For example, rather than enduring 10 percent unemployment during an economic downturn, a five-day work week could end at noon on Fridays, leaving enough jobs for everyone by working 10 percent less time. Productivity likely would drop by less than 10 percent because most people probably would work more efficiently if they had less time to complete their usual tasks. Increased productivity eventually would lead to economic recovery and full employment. If workers found they were happier with a shorter work week, the economy would not need to regain its previous level of output. Workers could simply continue to enjoy life more by working less. The process of implementing such government policies wouldn't be quite this simple, but the basic idea is to reduce employment for more people so fewer people will be completely out of work.

Nor would economic growth be necessary to accommodate the inevitable near-term growth in global population. In general, government policies could be redirected to creating more jobs from a given amount of economic output, rather than to generating more economic output with fewer workers. Most economic policies are a throwback to the early industrial era when the earth's resources seemed unlimited, workers were few, and the basic material needs of people were many. The objective was to increase total production by increasing productivity per worker, so that each worker would be able to earn more and spend more and promote even greater economic growth. Today, the earth's remaining natural resources obviously are limited, there are more workers than employment opportunities, and material well-being is no longer the limiting factor to the happiness or quality of life for many people of the world. Today, the need is to create more employment opportunities from less material and energy throughput or use.

Full employment of a growing population would not require return-ing to labor-intensive production or human drudgery. It would only require turning the attention of the economy to producing things that depend more on uniquely human thinking—creativity, imagination, insight, and intuition. More sophisticated mechanisms only employ "nonthinking" people in fewer numbers in the process of mass producing more economic output. Industrial mass production seemed a logical vision for the past, but it is not a logical vi-sion for the future. National and global economic policies should reflect the real needs of the future, not the false promises of the past. Global population eventually must stabilize at some sustainable level; the challenge of the future is to provide the *quality* employment opportunities necessary to help make population stabilization a reality.

Postindustrial public policies should be based on the premise that em-ployment opportunities are too important to the overall well-being of society to be left to the economy. Even in the most efficient of economies, economic value is determined at the consumer level, by the amounts that consumers are willing and able to pay for the things that workers are willing and able to produce. The economy places no value on the "quality of the work experience" for the worker, instead valuing only the quantity and quality of the products resulting from the production process in which workers participate. A major portion of a worker's total life experience is spent in the workplace, and as a consequence, the quality of one's work life has a major impact on one's overall quality of life. Government employment policies should not only focus on the quantity of employment opportunities but also the quality of employment opportunities. Workers should have access to stimulating work environments that allow them to develop their full potential for the creativity, imagination, innovation, and personal fulfillment necessary for sustainable prosperity. As-surance of a safe and healthful working environment, while necessary, will not be sufficient to sustain prosperity without growth.

Revenues to Sustain Prosperity

Sustainable economies must be supported by sufficient tax revenues to support the essential economic functions of government. Today's tax structures in the so-called market economies are designed to support economic growth rather than sustainability, using tax credits and government subsidies to promote natural resource extraction and investments in growth industries. Investment tax credits and lower capital gains tax rates leave much of the financial burden of government on middle-income taxpayers, who have little to contribute to economic growth other than their labor. In a sustainable economy, the burden of taxation would be shifted to discourage natural resource depletion, environmental pollution, and worker exploitation. In a sustainable economy, tax revenues would be used to promote resource protection, ecological restoration and regeneration, worker training, education, and empowerment. In general, taxes to discourage exploitation of nature and society would be used to provide incentives for the necessary transition to a steady state economy.

Solar energy eventually could provide the *ultimate* source of all tax revenue needed to fund the essential functions of government. Taxes on incomes and inheritances should be retained, but only for the purpose of redistributing income and wealth within and among generations. The natural resources of the earth are not the legitimate private property of any individual or nation. Individuals and nations, at most, can only be granted limited-use rights to the earth's resources. These limited-use rights should be accompanied by responsibilities for stewardship of nature for the long-run good of the whole of nature, including the future of humanity. The lack of sustainability in today's global economy is largely a consequence of the earth's biological and mineral resources, including fossil energy, being treated as marketable commodities. The resources of nature, including solar energy, belong to the whole of the earth, not to any individual, nation, or even uniquely to the human species. The human species, however, has the power to use these resources in ways that either enhance or diminish the well-being of all life on Earth, including human life. With power comes responsibility.

Solar energy is the ultimate source of all life, including the ultimate source of all economic value. The value of solar energy could be collected by governments, on behalf of the people, and used to support the essential functions of government. Collection, storage, and distribution of solar energy could be treated as a public utility, with net revenues from the sale of energy from solar sources used to support essential government functions, through licenses, fees, or taxes on energy sequestration. It is therefore essential that solar energy not be allowed to become an economic commodity. To ensure economic sustainability, solar energy must remain a common resource to be used to enhance life on Earth, including human happiness and well-being.

Economic Sustainability: Not a Sacrifice but an Opportunity

Economic sustainability will not be a sacrifice but instead an opportunity. The human experiment of the industrial era brought many material benefits to humanity. No one would choose to return to or remain under the preindustrial economic conditions that deny people even the basic physical necessities of life. However, a sustainable economy need not deny anyone of the economic necessities such as food, clothing, shelter, health care, or even many of today's leisure activities and luxuries. Developing nations can achieve the sustainable levels of economic development necessary for happiness and well-being without suffering the negative ecological and social consequences of industrialization. Developed nations can use their current economic surpluses to repair and restore the damage resulting from industrial economic development, without sacrificing the economic necessities of a more desirable quality of life.

Individual happiness depends on maintaining a healthy balance among efficiency in the use of time and energy, resilience to endure the inevitable shocks and disappointments in life, and continual renewal of the body and mind and regeneration of the human species. The essential characteristics of happy individuals and societies are the essentials of economic sustainability. Markets can provide efficient and effective means of meeting essential impersonal, individual, economic human needs, if their capabilities and limitations are recognized and respected. Meeting the basic economic needs of individuals within societies is a prerequisite for human happiness as well as economic sustainability. The essential functions of government—economic and social autonomy and equity—are as essential for human happiness as they are for economic resilience and regeneration.

While the steady state economy is a useful model for the future, the earth and life on Earth will never achieve a steady state, at least not unless the earth ultimately degrades to an absolute state of entropy—meaning no remaining useful energy, no economy, no life, nothing but a dead, inert mass. As long as there is life on Earth, there will always be cycles of light and darkness, birth and death, growth and decay. Human knowledge of the universe—the earth, humanity, society, and economics—will always be changing and evolving with the evolution of life on Earth. There will always be opportunities for progress and greater achievement for any individual within any society, any society within humanity, and humanity itself, for as long as solar energy continues to enter the earth's atmosphere, unless humanity allows the earth to continue to degenerate toward a state of entropy.

Happiness Has No Limits

There are no limits to human happiness and well-being once humanity rejects the failed hypothesis or notion that happiness depends on ever-greater income, wealth, and economic growth. Happiness is a natural consequence of living in harmony with the basic laws of nature—of respecting the hierarchies of sustainability and intentionality. Human intentionality must be directed toward working through the informal and formal processes of society to protect both society and nature from economic exploitation. The "hierarchy of happiness" is no different from the hierarchy of intentionality. Happiness has essential individual, social, and ethical dimensions. The individual cannot find happiness without respecting the basic social principles of human relationships, and societies cannot find happiness without respecting the basic principles of nature, including human nature. The essential principles of sustainability are the essential principles of human happiness.

Respect for the ecological principles of holism, diversity, and interdependence—in economic, social, and ecological relationships—is essential for happiness for individuals and societies. Respect for the social principles of trust, kindness, and courage—in economic, social, and ecological relationships—is essential for happiness for individuals and societies. Likewise, respect for the economic principles of scarcity, efficiency, and sovereignty—in economic, social, and ecological relationships—is essential to happiness for individuals and for societies.

The quest for economic sustainability is not about going back to the past; it is about going forward to a new and better era of human progress and prosperity. It is about creating a new and better world for the future. The essential mission of economic sustainability is to create opportunities for a desirable quality of life, a life of happiness, for all people of the world, now and for future generations.

A sustainable economy must provide permanent sustenance for the individual, social, and ethical well-being of all, including those of the future. It must enhance the physical and mental health of individuals. It must promote the economic and social health of families, communities, and societies. It must sustain the productivity and ecological health of nature. And it must provide each generation with the means of fulfilling its ethical responsibilities for the future of humanity. The creation of such economies is the essential challenge of economic sustainability. It is a challenge that can be and must be met.

Study and Discussion Guide for Individual Readers and Group Leaders or Instructors

- Find credible estimates of the current size of your national economy and calculate the size of your national economy one hundred

years from now, assuming it grows at an average rate of 3 percent per year: (Current economy) multiplied by (1+0.03) to the power of 100; $CE \times (1+0.03)^{100}$
- Search the Internet or library for a culturally appropriate reference that addresses the concept of a "steady state economy" and "prosperity without growth."
- Search the Internet or library for at least three different culturally appropriate references to happiness or quality of life. At least one of these references should relate to historic philosophies of happiness. At least one of these references should address the relationships between increasing income or wealth and increasing quality of life.

Questions for Individual Reflection or Group Discussion
- Do you believe economic growth is sustainable? Why or why not?
- Do you believe happiness or quality of life is dependent on income or wealth? Why or why not?
- Do you believe global population can be stabilized at a sustainable level? Why or why not?
- In what ways do you think your government's policies would need to be changed to address the mission of happiness rather than economic growth?
- Do you believe growth in human happiness or quality of life is sustainable? Why or why not?
- Why are your answers to these questions important to the people of your nation, your community, and to you personally?
- After thinking about these questions, what might you do differently to make life better, for others and for yourself?

Annotated Bibliography

Chapter 1. The Essential Questions of Economic Sustainability

Ikerd, John. *Sustainable Capitalism: A Matter of Common Sense*. Bloomfield, CT: Kumarian Press, 2005.

In *Sustainable Capitalism* Ikerd explains the process by which capitalism in the United States has degenerated into corporatism, from an economy guided by more or less free markets to an economy controlled by corporations. The basic concept of sustainable development, introduced in chapter 2, is used to explain why a capitalist economy, unrestrained by either society or government, is not economically sustainable. Chapters 3 and 4 address some of the essential questions of economic sustainability that are discussed in *The Essentials of Economic Sustainability* (*EES*). Chapter 3 gives credit to the efforts made by economists to address the negative ecological impacts of economic development but also points out the inadequacies of ecological economics. A sustainable capitalist economy would need to be fundamentally different from the capitalist economies that dominate the global economy today.

Readers who are familiar with the economic and political system of the United States might find *Sustainable Capitalism* useful in gaining a fuller understanding of the principles and concepts in *EES*. The book is basically an elaboration and application of the basic principles and concepts in *EES* from a uniquely American perspective.

Korten, David C. *When Corporations Rule the World*. 2nd ed. Bloomfield, CT: Kumarian Press, and San Francisco: Barrett-Koehler Publishers, Inc., 2001.

Korten's book makes a compelling case that corporations will invariably use their economic power to gain political power, which they then use to remove political restraints to still greater economic and political power. He documents the rise of corporate power in America and its negative impacts on American democracy. Korten sees the current global economy as a manifestation of corporate colonialism, with giant, multinational corporations spreading their economic and political power around the world. The economic interests of a relatively small group of extremely wealthy corporate stockholders now dictate both global and economic policy.

When Corporations Rule the World might help readers of *EES* to better understand the consequences of allowing decisions that affect the future of humanity to be made solely on the basis of economic values. Economic values are inherently impersonal and instrumental and thus place a priority on the present over the future. Large, publicly traded corporations are the epitome of enterprises that are driven by economic self-interest.

Marx, Karl, and Fredrick Engels. *The Communist Manifesto*. 1848. Reprint, New York: Simon & Schuster, 1964.

Marx's nineteenth-century book provides the classic and timeless explanation of the natural and irresistible tendencies of the capitalist class to exploit the working class in the pursuit of narrow, individual economic self-interests. Marx saw capitalism as a class struggle, where capitalists appropriated wealth created by, and rightfully belonging to, the laborers who transform natural resources into things of economic value. He apparently did not anticipate the degeneration of capitalism into corporatism but probably would not have been surprised by it. However, he did foresee the recent spread of capitalism to the far corners of the earth, where multinational corporations use their economic power to exploit the workers and natural resources of less economically developed countries.

Readers of *EES* might find *The Communist Manifesto* useful in gaining a fuller understanding of the natural forces that cause unrestrained capitalist economies to degenerate into extraction and exploitation. Marx's dire predictions regarding the future of capitalism seemed exaggerated, if not completely unfounded, until the mid-twentieth century, because social and political interventions had restrained the economic power of capitalists. Developments since then have validated Marx's hypothesis concerning the consequence of capitalist economies in the absence of adequate social or political restraints.

Schumacher, E. F. *Small Is Beautiful; Economics as if People Mattered.*
    London, UK: Bond & Briggs, 1973.
Schumacher's classic book begins with a clear explanation of why an economy
based on extraction and exploitation is not sustainable. He explains that the
belief in a limitless potential of economic production is a consequence of a
failure to recognize that current levels of production have been achieved only
by mining the nonrenewable resources of nature. He points out that society
ultimately must be sustained by renewable income, meaning renewable energy,
not the extraction and depletion of nature's wealth or natural resources. He
believes the problems threatening the sustainability of economies are primarily problems of scale—too much control and economic power concentrated
among too few economic entities.

In *Small Is Beautiful,* readers of *EES* might find a realistic alternative to
Marx's vision of communism: a collection of communities within which people
have the freedom to pursue their individual self-interest, but within which individuals are restrained by a commitment to the common good. Schumacher
provides a compelling vision of the possibilities of economic sustainability as
the only logical alternative to unsustainable economic growth.

Chapter 2. The Essential Hierarchies of Economic Sustainability

Ahl, Valerie, and T. F. H. Allen. *Hierarchy Theory: A Vision, Vocabulary and
    Epistemology.* New York: Columbia University Press, 1996.
Ahl and Allen give a thoughtful explanation of the fundamental relationships
among the various levels of organization within nested hierarchies. They review
the history of hierarchy theory and clearly articulate the differences between
"nested hierarchies" and hierarchies of domination or control. Perhaps most
important, the relationships between various levels within nested hierarchies
are interdependent, whereas the relationships within hierarchies of control or
domination are dependent, with lower levels being dependent and subservient
to higher levels.

Hierarchy Theory could provide readers of *EES* with a much more detailed explanation of the differences in roles and functions of the various hierarchal levels within nested hierarchies. For example, the authors explain why
higher levels are stronger and slower to change than are lower levels and why
the realization of possibilities by higher levels depends on lower levels. An understanding and acceptance of the principles of nested hierarchies is essential
to understanding many of the conclusions in *EES*.

Capra, Frijof. *The Web of Life.* New York: Doubleday, 1996.
Capra relates the concept of nested hierarchies to the hierarchal "networks" that make up all living systems. The various parts or components that make up the whole of living systems—organisms, organs, tissue, cells, etc.—are wholes within wholes that together form hierarchal networks or "webs of life." Although hierarchal relationships are not given a great deal of space in Capra's book, such relationships provide a conceptual foundation for his entire discussion on living systems.

The Web of Life might be particularly useful to readers of *EES* to help them understand the fundamental importance of hierarchal relationships in living systems, including societies and economies. A basic premise of *EES* is that current economies are not sustainable because they are inherently organismic, living systems that have been managed as mechanistic, nonliving systems.

Ikerd, John. *Sustainable Capitalism; A Matter of Common Sense.* Bloomfield,
    CT: Kumarian Press, 2005.
In *Sustainable Capitalism,* Ikerd addresses the hierarchies of sustainability in chapters 7 and 10. "The Three Economies of Sustainability," chapter 7, begins with an exploration of the ethical roots of sustainability in *deep* ecology. The ecological economy is the same as nature's economy, and it functions according to the basic principles of nature. The social economy functions within the ecological economy and the individual economy functions within the social economy. Chapters 8, 9, and 10 in *Sustainable Capitalism* focus on levels of decision making and organizational management that parallel levels of the hierarchy of intentionality in *EES.* Although the terminology is somewhat different in *Sustainable Capitalism,* the basic ideas are much the same as those in *EES.*

Sustainable Capitalism is an American elaboration or application of the basic principles and concepts in *EES.* It contains more examples and applications to specific economic and political situations. Readers who are familiar with the U.S. economic and political system might find this book useful in gaining a fuller understanding of the principles and concepts in *EES.*

Pawlowski, Artur. *Sustainable Development as a Civilizational Revolution.*
    London, UK: CRC Press, Taylor Francis Group, 2011.
Pawlowski addresses the hierarchal relationships of sustainable development from a slightly different perspective than in *EES,* but he draws essentially the same conclusions. He places the "ethical plane" at the highest hierarchal level;

the ecological, social, and economic planes at the second level; and the political, legal, and technical planes at the lowest level. Essentially, Pawlowski approaches sustainable development from the perspective of human intentionality, recognizing that ethical values shape the ecological, social, and economic decisions of humans. Political systems, legal structures, and technologies are means of implementing those decisions, thus placing them at a lower level within Pawlowski's hierarchy.

Readers of *EES* might find the chapters of *Sustainable Development* that address the "theoretical basis for sustainable development" and "philosophy, religion, and environmental education" particularly useful in gaining a deeper understanding of similar concepts in *EES*. These essential aspects of authentic sustainability are frequently omitted completely from discussions of sustainability or only mentioned briefly in other texts, while giving priority to nonessential issues instead.

Chapter 3. Ecological Principles Essential to Economic Sustainability

Berry, Thomas. *The Dream of the Earth*. San Francisco: Sierra Club Books, 1988. In this collection of essays, Berry addresses the relationships between humans and the earth from a variety of perspectives, in an apparent attempt to create a fuller and deeper understanding of the comprehensive and essential character of the nature-human relationship. In his chapter, "The Ecological Age," Berry addresses the ecological principles by which nature functions. He discusses diversity, hierarchy, and communion, meaning interdependence. Berry believes modern science is simply confirming what humans have known throughout history; humans are physically, socially, and spiritually connected with the earth.

The Dream of the Earth might be particularly useful to readers of *EES* who are interested in a more complete explanation of the interconnectedness between humans and nature and the ethical and spiritual dimensions of economic sustainability.

Capra, Frijof. *The Web of Life*. New York: Doubleday, 1996. Capra's *Web of Life* addresses several issues included in *EES*. In chapter 3, he explores ethical relationships between humans and nature through the concept of "deep ecology." In part two of the book, he relates the ecological principle of holism to "systems thinking." Capra also provides a summary of "Ecological Literacy" as an epilogue to his book. The ecological principles identified by Capra include "interdependence, recycling, partnerships, flexibility, diversity, and sustainability." Most of these principles are encompassed by essential ecological principles and characteristics of sustainable economies in *EES*.

The Web of Life might be particularly useful to readers of *EES* in understanding fundamental differences between living and nonliving systems. A basic premise of *EES* is that individual economic enterprises, overall economies, communities, and societies must be managed as living systems.

Daly, Herman E., and Joshua Farley. *Ecological Economics. 2nd ed. Principles and Applications*. Washington, DC: Island Press, 2010.

Daly and Farley's *Ecological Economics* addresses virtually all of the topics addressed in *EES*, in many cases, in greater specificity and detail. The topics related to *EES* are readily apparent in the two tables of contents. However, Daly and Farley assume the reader has a background in economics, or at least an intense interest in the field. *Ecological Economics* relies on various definitions and jargon of economics to achieve greater precision or specificity. That said, this could be a very useful reference for readers who want to delve more deeply into many of the topics included in the *EES*.

Ecological Economics might be most useful to readers of *EES* as a reference book to be used more or less as an encyclopedia. It might be a logical source to seek further information whenever the reader is sufficiently interested in a specific concept or topic in *EES* to stimulate further study.

Leopold, Aldo. *A Sand County Almanac*. New York: Oxford University Press, 1949.

In this classic book, Leopold explores the relationships between humans and natural ecosystems through his own personal experiences and observations as he relates to nature. He looks very deeply at the function of nature in a particular place, "A Sand County" in the state of Wisconsin, and draws conclusions that can be generalized to nature as a whole. In his essay, "The Land Ethic," he summarizes his observations: "Examine each question in terms of what is ethically and aesthetically right, as well as what is economically expedient. A thing is right when it tends to preserve the integrity, stability, and beauty of a biotic community. It is wrong when it tends otherwise." This essentially is the ethics of economic sustainability.

A Sand County Almanac might be useful to readers of *EES* in understanding that the integrity, stability, and beauty of a biotic community are all dependent on the essential ecological principles of holism, diversity, and interdependence. These are characteristics of mutually beneficial relationships among the diverse elements of living systems, of wholes. Leopold states the essential principles of ecological sustainability in terms that anyone who has spent some time in natural settings can easily understand.

Sale, Kirkpatrick. *Dwellers in the Land: The Bioregional Vision*. Athens: University of Georgia Press, 1991.

Sale begins his book by tracing the evolution of human thinking regarding the relationship between humans and the natural ecosystem. As he points out, in earlier times, humans have had great respect for nature, many civilizations viewing the earth as a living system of which humans are a part. It was only during the industrial era that humans came to believe they might eventually be able to declare their independence or ability to exist separate from nature. He observes how the thinking has come full circle with the emergence of the new ecological concept of "Ghea," the earth mother, which views the whole earth, including humanity, as a living organism. Sale identifies decentralization, mutuality, and diversity as basic principles of all natural living systems.

Dwellers in the Land might help readers of *EES* to understand "bioregionalism," meaning an attempt to create human societies and economies that conform to the principles of nature, as expressed in a particular region or geographic place. Bioregionalism essentially is the ecological dimension of human culture—the accumulated wisdom of generations who have lived in the same place within nature.

Tobias, Michael, ed. *Deep Ecology*. San Marcos, CA: Advant Books, 1984.

This collection of essays, by more than twenty different authors, provides a diverse perspective of the relationships between humans and nature. While some of the essays are very specific in nature, virtually all address the necessity of humans to conform to a set of basic principles by which nature functions. The focus on "deep ecology" in this collection emphasizes that understanding of and respect for the basic principles by which nature functions is not simply a matter of science; it is a matter of ethics and morality.

Deep Ecology might be useful to readers of *EES* in understanding the inviolability of nature's principles. They can be ignored but they cannot be violated without suffering the consequences. Whether individuals and societies respect the essential principles of nature ultimately depends of the ethical question: "Are principles of nature unchangeable and inviolable, or are they simply obstacles that can be overcome through human intellect and creativity?"

Chapter 4. Social Principles Essential to Economic Sustainability

Covey, Stephen R. *Seven Habits of Highly Effective People*. New York: Simon & Schuster, 1989.

Covey makes a compelling argument in the first chapter of *Seven Habits* that the basic principles of social relationships are just as valid and just as unchangeable as the basic principles of physics or chemistry. He points out the differences between social values, which are unique to specific communities or societies, and social principles, which are the same for all communities and societies. He also makes a compelling argument that positive social relationships depend on respect for such social principles. Covey places a high priority on the principle of trust and trustworthiness.

Readers of *EES* might find Covey's "habits" of "think win/win," "seek first to understand and then understood," and "synergize" particularly useful in comprehending how the ecological principles of interdependence or mutuality applies to human relationships. While Covey's book deals with individual behavior and personal relationships, it is equally applicable to communities, societies, and economies.

Kidder, Rushworth M. *Moral Courage*. New York: HarperCollins, 2000.

Kidder relies on surveys, focus groups, and personal interviews with people from widely different ethnicities, cultures, age groups, and educational and income levels to identify the five core values of social relationships referred to in *EES:* honesty, fairness, responsibility, respect, and compassion. He asked the various groups and individuals to identify the values that were held in highest esteem in their respective communities or social groups. While a large number of different values were mentioned among different cultures, the same five core values tended to be ranked near the top by all groups.

Moral Courage might be particularly useful to readers of *EES* who might not understand why courage is essential in maintaining positive human relationships. While the other principles probably seem obvious, courage may not. Kidder doesn't consider courage to be a core value; instead he sees it as being essential in realizing the social benefits of the other core values. Values and intentions accomplish little if anything without actions.

Putnam, Robert D. *Bowling Alone: The Collapse and Revival of American Community*. New York: Simon & Schuster, 2000.

Putnam focuses this book on the concept of "social capital," which is an attempt to emphasize the value of all forms of human relationships. Social capital includes both the economic and noneconomic value of human relationships. Social capital also includes the value of some "social" relationships that are arguably impersonal. If so, they are actually ethical rather than social. Social capital is not mentioned specifically in *EES* because discussions of social capital tend to focus on the economic value associated with social relationships. The social relationships most important for sustainability are personal relationships that evolve into cultural and ethical values. Such relationships reflect an aspect of true social capital that cannot be measured in economic terms or converted into economic value. The future of humanity depends on the expression of such relationships because their value is immediate, rather than deferred.

Readers of *EES* might find *Bowling Alone* most useful because of its extensive documentation of trends in social relationships during the twentieth century and the related trends in overall quality of life in American society. Overall quality of life appeared to improve during the first half of the century as social relationships grew stronger. Quality of life appeared to decline during the second half of the century as social relationships became weaker. Putnam leaves it to readers to draw their own conclusions regarding causes and effects.

Smith, Adam. *Theory of Moral Sentiments: The Glasgow Edition of the Works and Correspondence of Adam Smith.* 1759. Reprint, London, UK: Oxford University Press, 1982.

In this classic book, Adam Smith, the father of capitalist economics, focuses on the importance of human culture and social relationships as determinants of quality of life. He believed the essence of a person's sense of worthiness or self-esteem is largely determined through the nature of his or her relationships with other people. By moral sentiment, Smith was referring to the sense of rightness or goodness, or lack thereof, that people feel in their relationships with other people. He put a strong emphasis on empathy, or the ability to put oneself in the place of another, including the position of an "impartial observer." He felt that people should first ask how they would feel if they were the person thinking of taking a specific action, next how the person would feel who was affected by the action, then whether the person actually carried through with the action, and, finally, whether the greater good of society might be served by actions that were detrimental to individuals.

Many readers of *EES* might find *Theory of Moral Sentiments* surprising in that Smith believed the purely social and ethical value of human relationships far outweighed and overshadowed any tangible or economic value people might receive from their relationships with other people. He considered social justice to be of the utmost human value. He defined justice, at the very least, as one person not being allowed to benefit at the expense of another. Smith would undoubtedly consider today's "socially acceptable" extractive and exploitative economic behavior to be a violation of basic human justice. Adam Smith was a philosopher and social scientist first and an economist second. He clearly recognized and respected the hierarchy of intentionality.

Chapter 5. Essential Economic Principles of Sustainability

Case, Karl E., Ray C. Fair, and Sharon C. Oster. *Principles of Economics*. 10th
    ed. Englewood Cliffs, NJ: Prentice Hall, 2011.
This book is a basic introductory economics textbook. The economic principles addressed in *EES* are so basic they can be found in any good introductory economics text. However, such texts tend to define the concepts scarcity, efficiency, and consumer sovereignty, and then move quickly to analysis of supply, demand, and market price. Much of the emphasis in introductory economics textbooks is on giving students the language, economic jargon, and tools they will need to prepare them for higher-level courses in economics. In this regard, *EES* is very different from most economics texts.

    It might be worthwhile for readers of *EES* who have not taken an introductory course in economics to check out an introductory economics textbook from their local library, just to get a better idea of how the basic economic principles in *EES* fit in with conventional approaches to economic theory. *Principles of Economics* is an example of the type of book that might be most useful for this purpose.

Cole, Charles L. *The Economic Fabric of Society*. New York: Harcourt, Brace
    & World, 1969.
Cole provides a brief history of economic thought in terms that those with little or no previous knowledge of economics can understand. Although its focus is on the various economists who first wrote about economic concepts such as scarcity, efficiency, and sovereignty, it explains the concepts in more detail than is found in most more-contemporary economics textbooks. Cole defines scarcity as *the* economic problem, accepting the usual economic assumption that human needs and wants are insatiable, while natural and human resources are limited or finite. He uses this basic concept to define supply, demand, and efficiency, much as these concepts are explained in *EES*.

    Readers of *EES* might find this book particularly useful because it is written specifically for those with no previous understanding of the basic principles of economics. In addition, since it focuses on economic history, it provides a more comprehensive treatment of basic economic principles than do most current introductory economic textbooks.

Friedman, Milton, and Rose Friedman. *Free to Choose*. New York: Harcourt Brace Jovanovich, 1980.

In this book Friedman makes his most compelling case for the efficiency of free markets in allocating productive resources. While he fails to recognize, as do most economists, the existence of noneconomic value, he nonetheless provides valuable insights into the basic nature of economic value, efficiency, and consumer sovereignty. Friedman recognizes the legitimacy of government, particularly local government, in providing a means by which people can come together voluntarily to accomplish tasks they cannot accomplish individually. He is critical of government when those in power make laws that infringe upon the freedoms of individuals.

Readers of *EES* might find Friedman's book most useful to understanding the importance of sovereignty, the freedom to choose. An understanding of economic sovereignty is critical to understanding the importance of individuality and choice in meeting basic economic needs and wants. Economic sovereignty is also essential to realizing the potential benefits of trade, including international trade. However, the lack of sustainability in the current global economy is a reflection of Friedman's free market philosophy that trusts unrestrained individual economic choices to serve the greater good of society.

Heyne, Paul, Peter J. Boettke, and David L. Prychitko. *The Economic Way of Thinking*. 12th ed. Palo Alto, CA: Science Research Associates, 2009.

This introductory economics text provides more detailed explanations of basic economic concepts than can be found in most economic textbooks. Specific sections of the book focus on "Scarcity and Its Consequences," "Efficiency and Comparative Advantage," and "Substitutes Everywhere." All of these topics are addressed in *EES*, but not in the same depth or detail as found in *The Economic Way of Thinking*. Also stressed is the importance of sovereignty or freedom of choice as being essential in establishing economic value and achieving economic efficiency.

Readers of *EES* without a background in economics might find this book more useful than most other introductory economics texts. The authors do not rely heavily on charts and graphs to explain economic concepts but instead rely more on explanations and examples. This is probably one of the best economic texts available for those who want to gain a basic understanding of the issues addressed in contemporary economic theory.

Chapter 6. Essential Characteristics of Sustainable Economies

Capra, Frijof. *The Web of Life.* New York: Doubleday, 1996.
Capra's *Web of Life* probably provides the most comprehensive explanation available regarding the fundamental differences between living and nonliving systems. Capra's explanations are very similar to but in much greater depth than the discussion in *EES*. Capra also includes numerous examples and illustrations of the basic nature of living systems. He explains the importance of pattern, structure, and process for both living and nonliving systems, using examples and illustrations to highlight the differences. He focuses on the "self-making" nature of living systems as the most fundamental characteristic that differentiates living from nonliving systems.

Readers of *EES* might find *The Web of Life* most useful in understanding the importance of distinguishing between biological systems and mechanistic systems. Capra sees current mechanistic ways of thinking as intellectually and functionally obsolete and clearly inadequate to address the challenges of sustainability. Capra also integrates the two important concepts of systems thinking and living systems, both of which are essential to understanding sustainability.

Hock, Dee. *Birth of the Chaordic Age.* San Francisco: Berrett-Koehler, 1999.
Dee Hock was the founder of VISA Corporation, which he created as a "chaordic organization." According to Hock, it has since degenerated into a fairly typical financial corporation, but it was founded on the principles described in this book. Hock is very critical of the industrial paradigms of organizational management, which persist in spite of new management jargon designed to create the impression that organizations are responding to today's challenges. A chaordic organization functions as a holistic, diverse, interdependent living system. It is efficient but also resilient and regenerative. It is organized for a specific purpose and its purpose is reflected in a set of guiding principles. It has a dynamic structure that emerges and evolves to accommodate the purpose and principles of the organization. Individual members of the organization must have a shared vision and commitment to the purpose and principles of the organization if it is to function effectively.

Hock's ideas might be most useful to readers of *EES* in providing an example of a successful organization that was organized to function as a living, rather than mechanistic, organization. Obviously, organizational concepts alone are not sufficient to ensure economic sustainability—social and political restraints are also essential. Hock's "chaordic organization" nonetheless provides an organizational model that is completely compatible with the essential characteristics of sustainable economic organizations in *EES*.

Ikerd, John. *Sustainable Capitalism: A Matter of Common Sense*. Bloomfield,
    CT: Kumarian Press, 2005.

Chapter 6 in *Sustainable Capitalism*, "Managing the Sustainable Organization," provides a more in-depth description of the nature of sustainable economic organizations than is provided in *EES*. Industrial management theories and strategies are contrasted with theories and strategies necessary for economic sustainability. The concepts of "holistic management" and managing by the "triple bottom line" are used as examples of emerging management philosophies and strategies that are compatible with the essential characteristics of sustainable economic organizations. The emphasis in *Sustainable Capitalism* is on the principles of diversity, individuality, and interdependence as essential for economic sustainability.

Readers of *EES* who are familiar with the economic and political system of the United States and Western Europe might find this book most useful. While the examples and applications in *Sustainable Capitalism* are most relevant to market economies, the basic principles and concepts involved are relevant to all types of economies.

Senge, Peter M. *The Fifth Discipline: The Art & Practice of the Learning
    Organization*. New York: Doubleday, 1996.

In this book, Senge attempts to develop *systems thinking* as an academic discipline. He refers to organizations that are managed as living systems as "learning organizations." Such organizations have the capacity to continually learn, as a collective whole, and to use the new knowledge to renew, regenerate, redesign themselves. Senge identifies personal mastery, mental models, shared vision, and team learning as the core disciplines of learning organizations. The fifth discipline is systems thinking. His explanations of these core disciplines are essential to understanding the purpose and process of collaborative learning, which are essential to authentic sustainability. Senge uses a series of diagrams to demonstrate how continuous feedback loops can create patterns of acceleration, decay, and oscillation.

The Fifth Discipline might be most useful to readers of EES in understanding the nature and importance of systems thinking to sustainability. Senge uses the principle of leverage to explain how people can intervene in cases of reinforcing cycles or trends that are moving in negative or destructive directions. He also writes about the necessity for a shared vision among those involved in learning organizations to reverse negative tendencies and keep the organization moving in a positive direction.

Chapter 7. Essential Characteristics of Markets in Sustainable Economies

Case, Karl E., Ray C. Fair, and Sharon C. Oster. *Principles of Economics*. 10th
   ed. Englewood Cliffs, NJ: Prentice Hall, 2011.
The basic functions of markets addressed in this chapter can be found in any good introductory economic text. Most such texts use tables, charts, graphs, and examples to explain the various market concepts, which may be very useful for some readers. Specific topics in this text include "Input Markets, Output Markets," "Demand in Product Markets," "Supply in Product Markets," and "Markets and the Allocation of Resources." It may be worthwhile for readers who have not taken an introductory course in economics to check out an introductory economics textbook from a library just to get a better idea of how the basic market concepts and functions explained in this chapter of *EES* fit in with conventional approaches to economic theory.

   Principles of Economics is an example of an introductory economics textbook that readers of *EES* might find useful for either learning or reviewing some of the most basic ideas in economics.

Cole, Charles L. *The Economic Fabric of Society*. New York: Harcourt, Brace
   & World, 1969.
This book is written for those who have not had a previous course in economics, which makes it particularly useful in understanding the basic concepts and functions of markets. It includes sections dealing with "Economics as a Theory of Choice," "Opportunity Costs and Production Possibilities," "The Invisible Hand, Demand and Supply," "Competition and Its Benefits," and other market concepts addressed in this chapter of *EES*. Cole traces the evolution of Western economic thinking from Aristotle to the classical capitalism of Adam Smith, Malthus, and Ricardo, to contemporary neoclassical economics.

   Even though Coles's focus is on the history of economic thought, readers of *EES* may find his treatment of basic economic principles to be more comprehensive and easier to understand than explanations found in most current introductory economics textbooks.

Daly, Herman E., and Joshua Farley. *Ecological Economics, Second Edition: Principles and Applications.* Washington, DC: Island Press, 2010.

Virtually all of the topics addressed in *EES* are addressed in greater specificity and detail in Daly and Farley's *Ecological Economics.* The related topics should be readily apparent from the table of contents. Daly and Farley assume the reader has a background in economics, or at least an intense interest in the subject, and is thus either familiar with or willing to learn the various definitions and jargon that characterize economics as a profession. *Ecological Economics* is probably the most widely respected authority among academics and professionals on issues linking ecology and economics. It is also a credible source linking ethical and social issues to economics and ecology. Chapter 1 provides an excellent overview of the critical issue of sustainable economic development, without growth.

Ecological Economics might be a very useful reference for readers who want to delve more deeply into specific issues included in *EES.* However, *EES* allows readers to gain a basic understanding of the "essentials" of economic sustainable without the economic understanding and time commitment required to read and digest all of the issues addressed in *Ecological Economics.*

Heyne, Paul, Peter J. Boettke, and David L. Prychitko. *The Economic Way of Thinking.* 12th ed. Palo Alto, CA: Science Research Associates, 2009.

The authors provide more detailed explanations of basic functions of markets than can be found in most introductory economics textbooks. Specific sections of the book focus on "Opportunity Costs, Sunk Costs and Marginal Costs," "Comparative Advantage," "Uncertainty and Profits," and other market concepts and functions addressed in this chapter of *EES.* They do not rely heavily on charts and graphs but instead provide more detailed explanations and examples. This book is also more limited in scope than many other introductory economics textbooks, which allows it to focus on the more basic ideas in economics.

Readers of *EES* might find *The Economic Way of Thinking* particularly useful because it is one of the best economic texts available for those who want to gain a broad understanding of the basic issues addressed in contemporary economic theory.

Ikerd, John. *Sustainable Capitalism: A Matter of Common Sense.* Bloomfield, CT: Kumarian Press, 2005.

Ikerd provides a more in-depth description than is provided in *EES* of conditions and consequences of economic competition, operational efficiency versus allocative efficiency, international free trade, comparative advantage, opportunity costs, and other basic market concepts. *Sustainable Capitalism* also addresses the evolution of free market capitalism from the time of classical economists, such as Adam Smith, and neoclassical economists, such as Milton Friedman. In this book, Ikerd also defends the necessity for competitive markets in sustainable economies, regardless of whether the economies are called capitalist or socialist.

Readers of *EES* may find the explanation of the evolution of capitalism to corporatism useful in understanding why global market economies no longer function as classical market economies, regardless of widespread claims to the contrary. The emphasis in *Sustainable Capitalism* is on restoring economic competitiveness to market economies as a means of restoring credibility to market economies.

Chapter 8. Essential Functions of Government for Economic Sustainability

Case, Karl E., Ray C. Fair, and Sharon C. Oster. *Principles of Economics*. 10th
    ed. Englewood Cliffs, NJ: Prentice Hall, 2011.
The role of government policies in regulating markets is also covered in most introductory economics textbooks, such as this one. Some of the government-related sections in this work include "Market Imperfections and the Role of Government," "Public Finance: Externalities and Public Goods," "The Economics of Taxation," and "Growth, Productivity, Employment and Taxation." All of these discussions rely on examples related to U.S. economic and government policies.

Principles of Economics is an example of an introductory economics textbook that readers of *EES* might find most useful to learn or review some of the most basic ideas in economics regarding the essential functions of government.

Daly, Herman E., and John B. Cobb. *For the Common Good: Redirecting the
    Economy toward Community, the Environment and Sustainable Future*.
    Boston: Beacon Press, 1989.
Daly and Cobb point out that the Greek root word for economics, *oikono-mia*, refers to stewardship of all natural and human resources for the overall well-being of the household, society, and natural environment, rather than the current meaning of economics as a means of managing only scarce resources for the impersonal, instrumental benefit of individuals. The book focuses on the policies and functions of government necessary to secure stewardship of all

resources to ensure the long-run ecological, social, and economic benefit of society and the natural environment. The prescriptions suggested in the book are primarily government policies, but the authors make clear that effective public policies must be built upon public consensus.

For the Common Good might be most useful to readers of *EES* in linking government's responsibility for the common good of society and humanity to the concept of ecological and economic sustainability. Daly and Cobb brought social justice and ethics into public discussions of sustainability. Prior to this book, sustainable development was thought of primarily as an environmental or natural resource issue.

Daly, Herman E., and Joshua Farley. *Ecological Economics, Second Edition: Principles and Applications.* Washington, DC: Island Press, 2010.
A comprehensive discussion of the various functions of government and alternative public policies related to economic sustainability can be found in *Ecological Economics*. Daly and Farley assume the reader has a background in economic policy, or at least an intense interest in government policies related to the economy, and is thus either familiar with or willing to learn the various definitions and jargon that characterize the economics profession. "Cap and Trade," "Polluter Pays," and "Pigouvian Taxes" are just a few examples of popular public policy options among ecological economists. *Ecological Economics* also includes an extensive section on basic macroeconomic concepts, such as the "creation of money," "fractional reserves," "and monetary and fiscal policy."

For readers of *EES* who want to delve more deeply into specific economic functions of government or specific types of public policies, *Ecological Economics* might be a very useful, authoritative reference.

Heyne, Paul, Peter J. Boettke, and David L. Prychitko. *The Economic Way of Thinking.* 12th ed. Palo Alto, CA: Science Research Associates, 2009.
The Economic Way of Thinking includes several sections related to the basic functions of governments and public policies. Some of the sections most relevant to chapter 8 include "Price Setting and the Questions of Monopoly," "The Supply of Money," and "Fiscal Policy, Monetary Policy, and Political Economy." The authors address these issues in terms that are more basic and easier to understand than in most introductory economics textbooks, with less emphasis on tools and economic jargon.

Readers of *EES* might find *The Economic Way of Thinking* particularly useful because it probably is one of the best economic texts available for those who want to gain a broad understanding of the basic functions of government and the essential role of public policy.

Ikerd, John. *Sustainable Capitalism: A Matter of Common Sense.* Bloomfield,
    CT: Kumarian Press, 2005.

Ikerd discusses the essential functions of government in much greater detail in chapter 8 of *Sustainable Capitalism*, using the United States as a specific example. He contrasts two competing philosophies of government: a means of ensuring private property rights and a means of ensuring equity and justice. He argues that the functions of ensuring social equity and justice are essential functions of government for economic sustainability. The issue of economic competitiveness—market structure, conduct, and performance—is also discussed in greater depth in chapter 10 of *Sustainable Capitalism* than in this chapter of *EES*. The distinction between public goods and collective good is discussed in chapters 9 and 10: "Managing the Public Economy" and "Managing the Private Economy."

Sustainable Capitalism likely will be the most valuable overall supplemental reference for readers of *EES* who are familiar with the U.S. government and its policies. As indicated in the study and discussion guide at the end of each chapter, *EES* was written with the assumption that readers would supplement the book with other references that are culturally appropriate and locally relevant.

Chapter 9. The Essential Mission of Sustainable Economies

Daly, Herman E., and Joshua Farley. *Ecological Economics, Second Edition:
    Principles and Applications.* Washington, DC: Island Press, 2010.

A comprehensive discussion of steady state economy can be found in Daly and Farley's *Ecological Economics*. Daly is perhaps best known for articulating the concept of a "steady state economy"; the emerging discipline of ecological economics is premised on this important concept. Daly and Farley assume the reader has a background in economics, or at least an intense interest in the subject, and is thus either familiar with or willing to learn the various definitions and jargon that characterize economics as a profession. *Ecological Economics* can be a very useful reference for readers who want to delve more deeply into the conditions and implications of a "steady state economy" and the possibilities of economic *development* without economic *growth*.

For readers of *EES* who want to delve more deeply into almost any concept addressed in this book, *Ecological Economics* probably is the most useful and authoritative reference available.

Easterbrook, Gregg. *The Progress Paradox, How Life Gets Better While People Feel Worse.* New York: Random House, 2003.
Easterbrook points out that practically all of the material and tangible aspects of life in developed nations has improved over the past several decades, but people in many such nations are no happier than they were fifty years ago. He tends to blame the failure of greater wealth to bring greater happiness on people's unrealistic expectations. Whenever increased wealth doesn't make people as happy as they expected to be, they become disappointed and depressed. However, he admits the growing lack of confidence in increased wealth as a means of achieving happiness relates to the fact that the pursuit of wealth does not give life a sense of purpose or meaning. He points to the disparity in wealth between developed and developing nations and suggests that people might be far happier if they shared the wealth they have with those in other nations who have so much less than if they continue the relentless pursuit of wealth.

The *Progress Paradox* might be most useful to readers of *EES* in understanding that history clearly indicates greater wealth does not necessarily bring about greater human happiness or satisfaction in life, regardless of the reason. Economic growth has not proven to be an effective strategy for sustainable human progress.

Ikerd, John. *Sustainable Capitalism: A Matter of Common Sense.* Bloomfield, CT: Kumarian Press, 2005.
Chapter 2 in *Sustainable Capitalism*, "The Pursuit of Enlightened Self-Interest," traces the historical transition from economics as the pursuit of overall well-being or happiness to economics as the pursuit of wealth. Classical economists, such as Adam Smith and Thomas Malthus, assumed that people would pursue their economic interests within the context of societies and cultures that would place social and ethical constraints on their pursuit of individual self-interests. The neoclassical era in economics, which began in the early twentieth century, eventually resulted in the abandonment of social and ethical dimensions of classical economics. The relationship between happiness and economic self-interests is also addressed in chapter 1 of *Sustainable Capitalism*.

Readers of *EES* might find these discussions in *Sustainable Capitalism* most useful in understanding that the pursuit of happiness does not require abandoning the concept of free markets as envisioned by classical economists such as Adam Smith. Economic sustainability will require a return to the classical concept of a market economy, with appropriate ethical and social bounds and restraints.

Jackson, Tim. *Prosperity without Growth: Economics for a Finite Planet.* Oxford, UK: Earthscan-Taylor Francis, 2011.

This book is based on a long-term project carried out by a number of distinguished scholars from a variety of academic disciplines. Their task was to explore the realistic possibilities of sustaining continual progress in prosperity or overall human well-being, without continual economic growth. They considered economic well-being to be but one dimension of the broader concept of prosperity, which includes social and ethical dimensions of well-being as well. Their basic conclusion was that while the transition from economic growth to prosperity without growth would not be quick or easy, it is nonetheless possible. A primary challenge is to sustain a level of economic activity that will meet the needs of society as well as those of individuals. However, there is no logical alternative to prosperity without growth, other than to accept the ultimate collapse of human civilization, since economic growth is not sustainable.

Readers of *EES* might find *Prosperity without Growth* to be the most compelling, authoritative, contemporary, and practical guide to redirection of national and global economic policy away from economic growth and toward economic sustainability. This could be one of the most important books of the twenty-first century.

McKibben, Bill. *Deep Economy: The Wealth of Communities and the Durable Future.* New York: Henry Holt, 2007.

In the first chapter of *Deep Economy*, McKibben clearly explains, in easy-to-understand terms, how the industrial era of economic development initially brought tremendous growth in human material well-being but has since begun to create more environmental and social costs than economic benefits. He also points out the failure of economic development to create greater human satisfaction or happiness. He confirms that there is no relationship between wealth and overall well-being beyond some modest level needed to meet basic human needs for food, clothing, and shelter and to allow the human body adequate rest and relaxation. McKibben points to ecological crises, such as global climate change and depletion of fossil energy, as compelling reasons why the economic growth rates of the industrial era are simply not sustainable.

Readers of *EES* might find *Deep Economy* most useful in understanding the futility of continuing to emphasize growth as the mission of economic development. The book also explains the real possibilities of creating a fundamentally better economy and society beyond sustainability.

Wilkinson, Richard, and Kate Pickett. *The Spirit Level: Why Greater Equality Makes Societies Stronger.* London, UK: Bloomsbury Press, 2009.

Wilkinson and Pickett provide a variety of statistics comparing various indicators of quality of life among more than twenty "developed" nations and among the various states within the United States. They then correlate quality-of-life indicators with a measure of "income inequity" across nations and states. The correlations clearly show that quality of life is more closely correlated with social and income inequity among people within different nations and states than within absolute levels of income or wealth. Some of the wealthiest nations and states rank among the highest in quality of life, while others of the wealthiest rank among the lowest in overall quality of life. Even physical indicators of well-being, such as health and longevity, tend to be more positive for nations and states with greater social and economic equity.

Readers of *EES* may find this book most useful in understanding that beyond some modest level of economic well-being, social equity and justice become far more important than economic growth as a means of improving the overall quality of life within a society. Readers in the so-called "developed nations" may be surprised at how low their affluent nations rank in overall well-being, and readers in the so-called "developing nations" may be surprised at how little economic income and wealth is actually required to achieve a desirable quality of life.

Index